ALLEY

VOUVRAY •

• AMBOISE

CHER

• CHENONCEAUX

•LOCHES

TROUBLE BREWING IN THE LOIRE

Also by Tommy Barnes

A Beer in the Loire

TROUBLE BREWING IN THE LOIRE

Tommy Barnes

MUSWELL
PRESS

First published by Muswell Press in 2021
Copyright © Tommy Barnes 2021
Recipes © Tom Mathews

Typeset in Bembo by M Rules
Printed and bound by CPI Group (UK) Ltd, Croydon CR0 4YY

A CIP catalogue record for this book
is available from the British Library

ISBN: 9781916360259
eISBN: 9781916360266

Muswell Press
London
N6 5HQ
www.muswell-press.co.uk

To Rose

RECIPES

CHAPTER 1

'Hi, guys. Firstly, thanks for coming to our first ever Braslou Bière marketing meeting. Actually, let's call it a thought tinkle. An ideas slurry. I appreciate some of you had to reschedule other meetings.

'Albert, you'll take the minutes, seeing as you've got a crayon. Shall we go around the table and introduce ourselves?'

Albert, strapped into his baby seat at the end of the tiled table in front of the grand fireplace in our large, high-ceilinged French country kitchen, regarded me curiously as he chewed a piece of banana.

'Errr, Daddy. You a potato man,' said Albert, aged two and a bit.

'I'm a potato man? Good. Rose, would you like to kick off?'

'We're just having breakfast, Tommy. This isn't a marketing meeting.'

'Good. OK, in that case I'd like to bounce a few slogans off you. Likewise, if you have any of your own, feel free to shout them out.'

Albert put his yoghurt bowl on his head. 'Erm. You're sausages, Daddy,' he said.

'Good. OK, how about this one – *Think. Drink Braslou Bière.*'

'You've just stolen the *Think. Don't Drink and Drive* slogan, except you're trying to encourage people to drink. That's awful. The more I think about it, the more awful it is. You can't use that,' said Rose, taking a decisive slurp of cappuccino.

'Good. OK. We'll scrap that one. But that's what these meetings are all about though, isn't it? Fleshing out ideas.'

'It's breakfast, Tommy. It's not a marketing meeting.'

'OK. How about this one? *Braslou Bière – Yeah, It Cocking Did.*'

'What does cogging mean, Daddy?' said Albert.

'Never mind, Albert. It's a positive message. The kids will think we're cool. It's daring and a little bit mysterious, which is one of our brand values.'

'Some points – A: you're not trying to sell beer to the kids. B: you mustn't sell beer to the kids. C: what does it even mean? And D: we have brand values?' said Rose.

'All valid. We'll put that down as a possibility.'

'Oh, and E: can we not say "cocking" in front of Albert?'

'Valid. Good. Note that down, Albert.'

'Cogging, cogging, cogging,' said Albert.

'Good. OK, how about *Braslou Bière – Born in a Barn.*' – I glanced at Rose, who looked confused but not disappointed – '*Like Jesus.*'

Rose sighed. 'Offensive to literally billions of Christians worldwide. And this is still a traditional Catholic country. The French will have you deported.'

'Good. Albert, let the minutes state that Mummy thinks it needs work.'

'I what? You can't use it, Tommy. It's a massive no,' said Rose.

2

'Err, Daddy, you're an ice cream,' said Albert.

'Good. Fine. OK, final one.' I checked my notes. '*Braslou Bière – Shits on Other Beers.*'

'Shid cogging shid cogging shid cogging,' said Albert.

'Tommy, don't swear in front of Albert. You can't have a swear word in your slogan.'

'Yes, but this is the genius of it. It's punchy, which is one of our brand values, and it's mildly offensive, which is also one of our brand values. But best of all, it's basically the old Carlsberg slogan – *Probably the Best Lager in the World* – but with a twenty-first-century twist, and by that, I mean it has swearing. That slogan worked wonders for Carlsberg and they didn't even have swearing. Imagine what it could do for us.'

'Firstly, it's not mildly offensive. It's downright offensive. You couldn't have that on posters or business cards. Your clients would be furious. Secondly, it's against the law. You can't swear all over your marketing materials. You'll get arrested. It's an absolute no.'

'Ah. Good. Right. You sure it's illegal?'

'Yes. They'll prosecute you. You'll get fined.'

'Good. How big a fine hypothetically speaking?'

'I don't know. Ask Fred the policeman.' (One of the nice things about rural France is you still have a local policeman.) 'Why are you looking so worried?'

'Hey, this apricot jam is less orange than I remember previous jams to have been,' I said.

'Tommy, you're changing the subject.'

'Albert, have you noticed the jam?'

'Cogging jam. Errm, you're a cogging shid, Daddy,' said Albert.

'Tommy, you haven't had anything printed with *Shits on Other Beers* have you?' said Rose.

3

'God no.' Of course I hadn't. Jesus, Rose. Have some confidence in me, for Christ's sake. I mean, yes, OK, I'd had it printed across the back of the van – guilty as charged, your honour – but I hadn't used it on any of my promotional materials yet so there was no real problem. Come to think of it, I had given Bruno a poster for his restaurant in Braslou with the slogan on but, you know, it was quite hard to read. It was certainly not on my business cards, so there was really nothing to worry about. I would just have to make sure I reversed the van against the brewery for the rest of my life so the police and, more importantly, Rose wouldn't ever see it.

'Oh, by the way Tommy, Scott and Elena called. Can you put some beers aside for them at Richelieu market tomorrow? They want to give them to the guests at their gîte.'

'Ah. Ordinarily yes, Rose. But I'm not going to Richelieu market tomorrow, so I can't.'

Richelieu is the nearest town to our village of Braslou in the Indre-et-Loire, central France. We'd moved here four years previously to escape the perpetual crush of London and to start a new life making artisanal beer and sculptures and generally being insufferable.

'Why not? You've got loads of beer in stock and August is peak season.'

'Why am I not going to the market? Oh yes. Excellent question, Rose. Why on earth would I not go to the market? Well, let me enlighten you, Rose. I'm not doing the market, *Rose*,' – I started saying her name as if I wasn't convinced it was her real name, even though I had been in a relationship with her for seven years and we were married and therefore I was pretty certain it was – 'for the simple reason, *Rose*, seeing as you seem to be the expert, *Rose*, for the simple reason that

'I've surrounded my brewery in two metres of wet concrete and I can't get into it to get my stock.'

'You've what? You've done what? You have got to be kidding me, Tommy. You didn't take the stock out before they started the concreting? But surely that's just common—'

'I'm going to stop you right there, *Rose*. You wouldn't know this because you are not a *brewer, Rose*,' – now I emphasised 'brewer' like it was an occupation ever so slightly more important than a brain surgeon – 'but surrounding one's *brewery* with two metres of wet concrete is one of the most common challenges us *brewers* face.'

'No other brewer has ever done that. I guarantee they haven't.'

'Look, *Rose*, let's not start accusing people of being wrong or right. It's the modern world, *Rose*. There is no wrong or right. It's called existentialism or Trumponomics or something, and I, for one, am all for it.'

'This is the most stupid bullshit I've ever heard.'

Rose was right. It was the most stupid bullshit she'd ever heard. And yet it was true. The brewery, situated in the old sandstone barn the other side of our garden, was surrounded by wet concrete. It was like St Michael's Mount when the tide was in. I was in the process of having a concrete area laid down in front of the brewery so that I could move pallets and things like that around. I mean, it wasn't a big deal. I could do next week's market, for God's sake, *Rose*. All it really showed was that the Braslou brewery was modernising. And modernising is a good thing, isn't it, *Rose*? I'm talking to myself now. Anyway, more of that later. We need to talk about French pop music.

There are several genres of French pop: There's Vanessa Paradis, of course, she's about 30 per cent of it. There's

Johnny Hallyday – even though he's dead, he still accounts for about 30 per cent as well. And then there is my favourite genre – what I like to call *disappointabeat* – an endless turnstile of middle-aged men with just-longer-than-mid-length 'statement' hair swept backwards to draw attention away from their drooping jowls. Men dressed like a C&A window display from 1989 – jackets with the sleeves rolled up, God help you all. A club of forty-something groaners in ironed jeans trying to demonstrate to their daughters' friends that they've still got it. Guys with egos made of balloon reassuring each other it's OK that they're still lamenting teenage heartbreak when they should be singing about bad knees and erectile dysfunction. Songs surely all written by the same person, because each tune has the same distinctive fingerprint – hungover, whimpering, joyless, melancholy, flaccid, half-written sub-ballads called 'You're Here, I'm There' or 'You're Up, I'm Down' or 'You're Still a Teenager, I'm Forty-six' that leave you with nothing but a lingering sense of irritation akin to a stone in your shoe. There's a naivety in it, but not of the endearing kind. Instead it's annoying, like an adult who talks like a child. In fairness, nowadays they seem to have all but rid themselves of these guys. They're still around somewhere, I'm sure – stuck aboard a semi-deserted cruise ship in the Atlantic blurting out creepy propositions into a microphone decayed by Gitanes and teeth-whitening products. Today's French pop music is Europop and imitations of British and American pop artists. Still awful, though. I mean, the French lead the way in many arts, but French pop music is the pits. But that's France for you – tolerant.

It was August 2018 and, miraculously, the brewery was going well. it was finally starting to earn us a crust. That's not to say I hadn't had some issues. I'm generally regarded as the first brewer to make a beer that tasted of bin juice, for example. The concrete debacle was yet another feather in my dunce's hat, but you know, generally things were good.

All the pressures of the last year (as masterfully documented in the seminal book *A Beer in the Loire* by a truly sensational writer and close personal friend of mine – ladies and gentlemen, I give you the fabulous Tommy Barnes!), starting a microbrewery in my barn in the middle of deepest wine country in France – despite not knowing how to brew beer – and at the same time having a baby and taking guardianship of Burt, the dog of Satan, among other lunatic animals, and trying to hack our way through peerless French bureaucracy using GCSE French from the mid-1990s. All that insane pressure was starting to ease. Yep, I was far, far too pleased with myself. As long as there were no more major life-changing events and the beer kept selling like this, we would be on easy street. I mean, Rose was seven months pregnant with our second child, but as I delighted in telling anyone who was foolish enough to enter my bore-off radius, 'The second child is much easier than the first.' I'd heard people say this before, and so I said it to other people as if I knew it to be true. No, we were finally starting to win at life, and it was all down to me. Well, mostly good fortune, an extraordinarily forgiving French public, a resourceful wife and a lot more good fortune, but also partly me. Now we were set up in the most beautiful old house in the little village of Braslou in Pays de Richelieu – Cardinal Richelieu's country – half an hour from the River Loire, brewing away to our hearts' content.

The house was built by a stone mason for himself in the late 1800s. It's a *maison de maître*, made from the white stone that is prevalent round here and which gives all the towns and villages a convivial glow. Being a *maison de maître* means even though it's not a huge house, it's grand in its way. A series of symmetrical, elongated rectangles, each space – the walls, the doors, the windows – so harmonious that it looks like it arrived on this piece of land, where the chalk of the escarpment runs into the sand of the Richelieu Forest, completely intact. It's a spacious house: each room has lofty ceilings latticed with perfectly regular beams, and no matter how long you live in it, it always feels airy. You can flounce into rooms and throw your arms in the air. You can swoon. It's that sort of house. You couldn't swoon in a two-bed semi in Maidenhead, you know what I mean? Here you can swoon. Outside, the front door is flanked by little bushes of bay and rosemary. The original wrought-iron fence and gateway knotted in wisteria run across the front, through which you can see to the left the modern, immaculate house and gardens of Monsieur and Madame Richard and, over the way, Damien and Celia's horse paddocks, behind which looms the dark of the Richelieu Forest. When we first left London for France, we rented the house for a month and fell in love with it, so when it came up for sale, we bought it immediately. That's how we ended up here. Before that we'd never heard of this area, the Pays de Richelieu.

It's not breathtaking, the Pays de Richelieu. It's not the volcanoes of the Auvergne or the valleys of the Dordogne or the jagged Brittany coast, but, BUT! – in July, when the sunflowers beam for miles across the gentle swells around Richelieu, when you pass alongside the noble wall of the erstwhile Château de Richelieu and across the way the angled sun of early summer's evening lights a mosaic of small fields pressed into the hills in 200 shades of green, occasionally separated by shocks of yellow from the last of the sunflowers, and then brilliant white where the chalk has been ploughed up, not a hedgerow to be seen save for shrub-lined waterways that pick their way along ancient boundaries. Those fields from a distance are marked out so cleanly, but as you get closer you see the rough edges that life brings: dusty, off-white smallholdings that have been there for ever, built in on themselves like miniature sandstone fortresses surrounded by well-kept *potagers* – neat vegetable patches comprised of lines of fat tomatoes, lettuces, cucumbers, courgettes, cornichons, aubergines, peppers. Or, alternatively, immaculate *maisons de maître* like our house – grand old mansions designed by architects who had mastered space and proportion. When you see the smallholdings and hamlets stuck like limpets on the hillsides, connected by ancient tracks patterned with spidery shadows from the branches of oak and fir trees, lined with orange sands, which criss-cross up and then back down the hill towards the village of Luzé, which is hidden in a hollow beside a tree-lined lake; or along the fir-tree forest, through Braslou to Marigny-Marmande, which twirls down towards the River Vienne; or to Faye-La-Vineuse (once the grand capital of the region, until it was usurped by the new town of Richelieu), which sits proudly on its summit on the hill above the Pays de Richelieu; or the road down to Châtellerault, which billows up and down like a shaken blanket. When every third or fourth field you pass has horses and ponies, sheep, little pig farms, cows, piled wood, parcels of forests – pine and oak, meadows of wildflowers. And when you stumble across the châteaux. The exquisite château at Corcoué, snuggled into the rise up towards La Tour-Saint-Gelin, which is so beautiful I thought it was a mirage when I first glimpsed it through the hills from the

9

top of the escarpment behind Braslou. The château down by the turning to the Île-Bouchard is almost its equal. Dozens of other châteaux. No one mentions these châteaux. They're not famous. They're just a part of the landscape. When you let yourself sink into the Pays de Richelieu on a July evening, then it is breathtaking.

We'd been in France for three years. In that time we had gathered an array of disparate creatures. There was Gadget the miserable miniature horse, Bella the mindless Cameroonian sheep, Nemo the little fighting fish, Louis the dog and, of course, his brother Burt, the hound of Satan. My nemesis. Almost certainly the bringer of my eventual downfall.

Gadget and Bella lived in the orchard behind our house on the edge of Braslou. There are cherry trees – some that give small, dark sour cherries and some that give fat, round, sweet red cherries. There is a plum tree and at the back, next to the old vines, are two apple trees that in summer are encircled by large, angry hornets.

Nemo lived in a bowl in the living room. Animals were constantly coming and going in our household. At one point we'd had two big woolly sheep. For a while we'd had little bantam chickens. Before Gadget we had a Shetland pony. I attributed all these acquisitions to Rose's pregnancy cravings, regardless of whether she was pregnant or not, because Rose first starting demanding animals when she was pregnant with Albert. I assumed a nurturing instinct had been awakened in Rose, but the thing was, even after she was pregnant, they continued to arrive. Some would get eaten, some would escape, some would be moved on for disciplinary reasons and yet more animals would take their place.

Now listen. People think I'm exaggerating about Burt

the dog, but if you really want an insight into his character, if you want a forensic examination of the crimes he has committed that day, you just have to study one of his poos. It's a timeline of depravity – a crescent-shaped record of sin, dotted with chewed pieces of children's toys, rinds of expensive cheeses stolen from tables, tax documents, radioactive waste, priceless artworks, fragments of Shergar's bones. You can plot his exact movements through his poo, and it's an insight into the dark world of a master criminal.

We'd had Burt for two years and for most of that time he'd been hell-bent on ruining my life in any way he could. He's a cross between a basset des Alpes and an Australian shepherd, a medium-sized, black, white and tan hound with the shape of an overinflated beagle. People look at him and think he's an adorable little overweight hound but actually, I'm pretty sure – and I don't say this lightly – I'm actually pretty sure he's a serial killer. In fact, I'm pretty sure all serial killers are connected to him. He is the puppet master. I can't prove it yet. *But Tommy,* I hear you say, *you're examining an animal's poo. Are you OK?* Well, maybe not.

At one point I'd managed to placate Burt for a few months by feeding him croissants and I thought maybe I'd turned things around. Recently, though, he'd started acting up even more than before. He had mutated like a virus. No matter how many croissants I gave him, he would still chew through chair legs and watch barely satisfied as I collapsed through the seat and onto the floor, or dig out the foam from the seats in the van so that I would eventually get piles, or break into the brewery and eat twenty kilograms of malt and leave vast, elaborate patterns of grainy dog shit all over the garden. I took him everywhere I could with me; it was a sort of masochism, I suppose – perhaps I wanted to be punished for previous sins. I don't know. Mostly I just wanted Burt to like me.

Damien, early thirties, dark curly hair cut short, was in my outbuilding, staring at a black pipe sticking out of the concrete floor with his hawkish, large, round, convincing eyes. Today his eyes were even larger and rounder than usual.

'Do you know what that is?' He said to me. His tone of voice expressed total disbelief. There was shock in his voice. There was a hint of something else. Anger maybe. Outrage. His world view had been exploded.

'No. I don't know what that is.' I lied. I did know what that was. As soon as I saw him staring at it I remembered it was there. This was not going to reflect well on the English.

'That is a water pipe.' Damien said it although it was almost as if he didn't believe his own words.

'Oh right. Well that's useful isn't it?'

'But, but Tommy—' Damien turned round and looked back across the garden. I looked too, although I really didn't want to. Stretching from one end of the once beautiful garden fifty metres over to where we were standing was a trench, three feet wide and four feet deep, banked on either side by big mounds of freshly dug earth. It was a bomb site. Walls had been obliterated to get the trench to where it was. Patios dug up. A mechanical digger sat, exhausted to one side. Mud tracks suffocated the once luscious grass. Damien had spent half the day in that digger digging a trench for me so I could lay down a water pipe all the way to the outbuilding. Now it appeared to Damien's astonishment, and to my shame because at one point I knew this but somehow I'd forgotten, that there was already a water pipe in the outbuilding.

Damien turned his glare from the garden onto me. He was disappointed with me. I thought for a moment he would turn violent.

'Oh, well.' He said. 'Let's go and have a beer.'

'Good idea.' I said. Damien knows me you see. He knows Braslou Bière, and he knows that this sort of total shit show, this theatre of the absurd is the very essence of what Braslou Bière is all about.

Damien and Celia are our neighbours. They live across the road with their daughters Colleen and Zoë. They've helped us in every aspect of our lives from the moment we moved in. Damien is tall. He is forthright in his talk and his actions. He's endlessly forgiving. He's the kind of man who if I didn't see him for twenty years, we'd still have the same relationship. We'd still be warm. Celia is slight and strong in the way people who ride horses are. She's tough and has an air of the aristocracy about her. She'd bend over backwards to help us out. They both would.

Over the course of three years I had developed four beers.

My blonde beer, Berger Blonde, named after our neighbours Damien and Celia Berger.

Then there was an amber beer called Biscuit Ale, made with honey.

Then Cardinal IPA – a take on a New England IPA but using all-European hops.

And finally a stout, confusingly called Clifton Porter, because it started out as a porter but then I started adding roasted barley to it, which for some people in the brewing world means the porter has become a stout. This is disputed, however, as, historically, stouts were just porters that were stronger or fuller bodied. Personally speaking, and this could blow the brewing world right open, I like to think the moment a porter really becomes a stout is when it has wrestled its first bear in the wild. Anyway, by the time my porter may or may not have become a stout I already had 8,000 labels that said Clifton Porter on them, so until the labels are used up, it's a porter and everyone else can fart off.

I bought my brewery from a guy in North Wales and installed it in the *dépendance* – the outbuilding on the other side of the garden to the house. It's not ideal – the floor doesn't drain, which makes it much harder to clean. The walls are crumbling. The mortar between the stones is falling out and I rather get the impression that that means creatures are moving in. The ceiling is low. Warped beams run across it. The summer before I'd started putting foil insulation up between the beams, but for reasons I can't fully explain, I've only managed half of the ceiling.

It's a 400-litre British brewery consisting of three large stainless-steel vats wrapped in insulation and wooden panelling, with heavy wooden lids, lined up along the wall opposite the door. It's powered with electricity. The three vats are called the kettle, the mash tun and the copper. The kettle is basically a boiler. It heats the water up to around 77–80° C. The strike temperature. The mash tun has a false bottom in it. I add my malt to the mash tun and then soak it in the hot water (known as brewing liquor) from the kettle so that it has a porridge-like consistency. I've already crushed the malt with my malt mill, which is powered by a drill I bought from Lidl. I normally mash the grain for an hour and a quarter. The idea is to convert the starch in the grains to sugar and pass as much of them as you can into the liquid. Then the liquid, now called the wort, passes through the false bottom and is pumped into the copper – the final vat. The copper is also a water heater. It has two giant elements at the bottom of it. I'll boil the wort for an hour or an hour and a half – the lighter the beer, the longer I'll boil it, because it's more susceptible to dimethyl sulfide, which can cause 'off' flavours. I add the hops at this stage. I tend to add hops at the start and end of the boil. At the start for bittering – hops contain alpha and beta acids that give the beer bitterness. I add hops at the end for flavour and aroma. The longer the hops boil, the more their aromatic oils evaporate and they lose desirable flavours.

The brewery is a spaghetti of metal pipes, pumps and plastic hoses, and at any moment some kind of liquid will burst out of the wrong pipe at the wrong time. Watching me brew is like watching a Homer Simpson montage.

Brew day is the best bit of brewing. A lot of running a brewery is a pain in the arse – especially when you're at my level, with a very basic brewery where everything is by hand. But brew day, with the smell of ground malt and a mystical aroma from boiling hops that all leads to the creation of a new beer, is fantastic.

Brew day: Berger Blonde

Malts
- Pale malt
- Wheat
- Biscuit malt
- Aromatic malt
- Melanoidin light

Hops
- Styrian Goldings

- Triskel
- Other additions
- Coriander seeds (crushed) in the boil

The best brew days start the day before. By that I mean if you can get the malt ground and the brewery all cleaned down and set up the day before, brew day itself is a relatively leisurely affair. You can get in early and if everything is already prepared, there's actually lots of down time in brewing. This particular day I hadn't done any of that, of course. This morning I had not ground my malt, and I had not cleaned the brewery and fermenter properly; I had not prepared in the slightest.

Firstly, I wrestled Albert into the car and drove him down the road to Annie and Claude's house. Annie and Claude are Damien's mum and dad, and Annie was Albert's nanny.

'*Salut*, Tommy,' said Claude.

'*Salut*, Claude. How are you?'

'I'm fine. Come and look at this.' Claude was stirring a big pot in the kitchen. I looked in. At first all I could see was liquid. Then something floated up from beneath the surface.

'Argh!' I leapt backwards.

Claude fished out a large, pink, gelatinous pig's ear.

'Pig's-ear stew. Delicious,' said Claude. 'I have some more pigs' ears if you want to take them back.' He pulled another couple of pigs' ears out of a bag and flapped them at me.

'No thanks, Claude.'

'Go on. Take them.' There was no way I was going to take them.

'Right. OK, thanks Claude.' Dammit.

Going to Annie and Claude's was an enriching experience for Albert. Annie looked after Damien and Celia's daughter Zoë, who was the same age as Albert. Annie didn't stand for any nonsense. She would get the kids outside to see the world. She'd take the kids to feed their chicks or the ducks. Claude would show them how to pacify a rowdy cockerel by locking its wings together or how to construct an exterior stone wall or hunt wild boar.

Once home with a bag of pigs' ears, I started grinding the malt. I hadn't had time the night before. I balanced my grinder on top of a black plastic bin and attached the Lidl drill to it. I set the drill to automatic and by that I mean I wedged a rock in between the handle and the trigger of the drill so that the trigger was permanently on, and as the fearsome teethed rollers began to turn, I shovelled malted barley into the hopper and watched as it slid down and was crushed to smithereens, as I would like all my enemies to have been. I stood next to the drill bathing in its thunderous machinations and imagining I was a futuristic Roman centurion riding it into battle.

Berger Blonde at this stage consisted mostly of pale ale malt – a standard light base malt and some wheat to give it more mouthfeel and head retention. Head retention is the amount of time the froth at the top of the beer stays before all the bubbles pop. The Berger Blonde is based loosely on a Leffe blonde beer. That was the starting point. It's a constantly evolving beer. All my beers are evolving.

I get my malts from a large maltings in Issoudun, a couple of hours east of us. The hops come mostly from the Alsace in eastern France and Germany.

Once the malt was ground, I chucked it into the mash tun and soaked it with water until it got to a porridge-like consistency and was at a temperature of around 65° C, a fairly standard temperature to mash at. The lower the temperature you rest your mash (within a range of 63–70° C), the more efficiency you'll get from your malt, but the thinner the beer will be. The higher you mash, the more mouthfeel you'll get with your beer, but you won't get as much alcohol from the grains. I had wheat in it, so I didn't need a really rich mash.

An hour in the mash tun, and then it was time to sparge out. This is where you pass the wort through the false bottom of the mash tun into the copper and rinse the grains with more liquor, until you have a wort in the copper with the right amount of sugar to give you the strength you want.

As I was sparging, the bell at the gate rang. It was my neighbour, Monsieur Richard. He'd brought over an enormous box of vegetables from his vegetable patch – the greatest vegetable patch in the Western world. An abundance of healthy-looking courgettes, cucumbers, tomatoes and bunches of parsley.

'*Salut,* Tommy. We'd like to invite you over for lunch on Sunday. I hear Rose is taking the children back to Britain for a few days. We don't want you to be all alone.' He knew that by day three I'd be sucking bits of old pizza crust up from down the side of the cushions with a straw. Whereas I avoided going back to the UK, Rose still went back whenever she could.

'*Salut*, Christian. Yes, I'd love to.'

'Brilliant. I think I've found somewhere for you to leave your malt as well. There's a methaniser at a farm over in Champigny-sur-Veude. The farmer there, Willy, says you can leave your spent malt there and he'll add it to the methaniser and turn it into reusable energy.' This was good news. After a brew I'm left with between fifty and a hundred kilograms of used malt. Often breweries will give the used malt to pig farms, but in my case the local pig farm was completely organic and my malt wasn't, so understandably they wouldn't take it. It meant I had to take it down to the dump, which seemed like a waste.

'You're a great man Christian. I–' I stopped talking because I saw a flicker of alarm in Monsieur Richard's eyes. He was looking behind me. Then a blur: something shot past in my peripheral vision and out onto the road. I could feel the air rush against me as it created a vacuum. Something with weight. Something capable of deadly force. It was a miniature horse.

'Ooh la la! GADGET!' I called after the horse as it bolted down the road, heading towards Richelieu.

A moment later a Cameroonian sheep followed. 'Ooh la la! Bella! Stop!' I screamed and headed after them.

I think it's a good measure of where I stand in the neighbourhood that, as I chased the miniature horse and a Cameroonian sheep down the road towards Richelieu in what must have seemed like a slow motion, absurdist remake of *Thelma and Louise*, a few of the local villagers driving by the other way didn't seem the least bit shocked. In fact, they just waved and grinned at me as if I was out for a Sunday stroll. It wasn't the first time Gadget had escaped, you see. In fact, all our animals were constantly absconding.

I cornered Gadget chatting up our neighbour Celia's horses down a little trail. Bella was hanging around cramping his style. Gadget thinks he's some kind of tall, muscled heart throb from the musical *Grease*. He doesn't realise that Celia's horses are three times the size of him. Or maybe he does and that's why he's so grumpy. Along with Monsieur Richard, I corralled him back into the garden and I reflected on a landmark occasion, my first genuine, spontaneous 'ooh la la'. You see, contrary to what we are led to believe in Britain, an 'ooh la la' doesn't have to be in response to something impressive. You can have angry 'ooh la la's – a car going too fast on your road, for instance; or you can have shocked 'ooh la la's – a miniature horse and a Cameroonian sheep making a break for freedom. I'm not sure how Gadget had escaped his enclosure in the orchard at the back. Someone or something had opened Gadget's gate. I mean, I knew it was Burt, but I couldn't prove it.

I got back into the brewery. The beer had over-sparged. That is to say, I'd passed too much water through the grains. There was a danger it would have stripped too much tannin from the husks of the grains, which would affect the quality of the beer. It was too late now. I'd have to hope for the best. I boiled the wort, adding my bittering hops – Styrian Goldings – at the start of the boil and adding some aroma hops – more Styrian Goldings, a French hop called Triskel, which is a floral hop, and some ground coriander seeds ten minutes before the end.

The next phase, once it's boiled, is to try and cool it down as quickly as possible and transfer it to the fermenter. I was aiming to chill the wort to about 17° C. The yeast I was using, a Belgian Abbaye yeast, worked best a little higher than this – 20–25° C – but I didn't really have any means of controlling the temperature in the fermenter, so my plan was to start off low and let the temperature rise naturally. The process of fermentation can raise the temperature of the wort by 10° C in some cases, so I hoped that by starting off under the optimal temperature range, it wouldn't end up too far over.

I have a plate chiller in my brewery. It works by passing cold water from the tap through it one way and the hot wort the other way. The heat transfers from the hot wort to the cold water, thus chilling it. If you think all this plate-chiller talk is boring, then to hell with you. There are whole swathes of society that get off on this stuff. There are middle-aged, bearded men climaxing at the very mention of a plate chiller all over the country. The problem with this sort of chiller is it can only chill the wort to a temperature relative to the temperature of the cold water coming in. The best my chiller could do was get the wort down to a few degrees above the temperature of the tap water. This was the height of summer, and the water from the tap – the water that I needed to cool my wort – was coming out of the tap at 18° C. I didn't have much choice. I chilled the wort to as low as I could – around 24° C – and pitched the yeast. Then I went out to curse at Gadget from a safe distance.

And that is how you brew Berger Blonde.

Madame Richard and Monsieur Richard – Marie-Thérèse and Christian, live opposite and to the left of us. They're in their sixties and seventies. Like Damien and Celia, they've been nothing but kind to us since we moved over. Monsieur Richard is a grand man. He has mastered life. Everything he does is done to the highest standard. His house is immaculate, his hedges so sharply carved you could slice your finger on them. Ever since I met him, he has been a role model for me. The way he acts, the way he works. I know if I could be like him, I'd be a success. Sadly, I'm nothing like him – hence Gadget the grumpy miniature horse escaping down the road on a regular basis.

The Richards often invite us over for lunch or dinner, and it's a window into traditional French life. There's no rush to get to the table. Monsieur Richard always starts by giving me a tour of his vegetable patch, a vast undertaking laid out with laser precision, populated with every vegetable the soil will allow to grow, all perfectly spaced and in straight rows.

When we finally sit down for aperitifs, Christian and I drink Coteaux du Layon, a sweet golden wine with tastes of pear and honey that comes from near Angers, a little to the west of us. Christian tops my glass up constantly, which in my mind is the mark of an excellent host.

On this occasion, a Sunday lunch, we barbecued outside. Monsieur Richard's son Denis had bought him a *plancher*. It's effectively a gas barbecue, but instead of a grill it has a solid bit of metal you cook on.

Marie brought out *saucisson* along with a little guillotine – a special *saucisson* cutter that could definitely take your finger off. I wondered if this was what Monsieur Richard used to cut his hedge. Marie gave us local melon and a tomato salad made from Monsieur Richard's *coeur de boeuf* tomatoes – enormous great things rippled like a Schwarzenegger bicep, the size of a grapefruit. Then Monsieur Richard cooked up strips of marinated pork that his grandson Alban, who works at the *charcutieur* in Richelieu had made. Alban was supposed to be at the lunch too, but his dad had gone away the night before, so he'd had a house party and was too hung-over to make it.

We finished with a box of delicious mini *pâtisseries*: fruit tartlets, cakes, éclairs and macarons. Marie insisted I eat at least sixteen of them and take the rest of them with me. There's still a ritual to the way the French eat, even when it's a relaxed lunch like this. There was concentration and seriousness to the way the table was laid out. Christian did the barbecuing, but Marie was in charge of most of the meal and it was important to her that it was as it should be. Most of my adult life has been spent getting lunch from sandwich shops. Food is food. But with Christian and Marie it's not.

As summer progressed, the quality of my beers started to deteriorate. I'd got away with over-sparging my last Berger Blonde, but I hadn't got away with the temperature of the fermentation. Indeed, I'd had the same problem with two previous beers I'd brewed in the heatwave. I couldn't keep the fermentation temperatures under control because my little brewery was housed in our barn, and the barn had holes in the walls, so the outside air came and went as it pleased and I couldn't really control the temperature in the brewery. Consequently, at the market, people had started telling me that my beer had 'character'. That might sound like a nice thing to say, but what they meant was it had character in the same way the guy down at the shopping precinct who wears a tutu and is perennially getting thrown out of Superdrug for eating the lipstick has character. My beers had developed some mildly undesirable flavours. At their worst they'd got a chemical aroma from the esters created from over-fermentation – a distinct smell of nail-polish remover. Also, I'd made an IPA with so many hops in it that I couldn't clear them from the beer. It turns out that if you have too many hop particles floating in your beer, it makes it explode when you open it. The gas bounces off them or something and the whole thing goes batshit. I don't know, I'm not a nuclear physicist, am I? But the number of carpets I ruined in 2018 was incalculable. And yet I didn't receive any dry-cleaning bills and people kept buying the beer, so what did I care? That's France for you – tolerant.

The concrete surrounding the brewery was dry by the time market day rolled round the following Friday, and I was back to selling reasonable amounts of increasingly dubious beer to the punters of Richelieu market and telling them that the second baby is easier than the first.

When you pull into the square in Richelieu, forty-five minutes south of the city of Tours, you think you've arrived in the capital. Lined by grand buildings, it's an extraordinary, walled, moated, Baroque new town built by Cardinal Richelieu (yes, him) in the seventeenth century. It's chiselled and crafted down to the last stone. The market has been going since the town was first built. It takes place on a Friday morning in the lower of the two main squares in Richelieu – the Place du Marché, which sits in front of the Église Notre-Dame – the large, classical, twin-spired church in the centre of Richelieu. The market starts in Les Halles, the vast, open-ended seventeenth-century market hall held up by a lattice of strong wooden beams, which runs from the dainty Place Louis XIII with its bandstand through to the big, open gentle concavity of the Place du Marché, the commercial hub of Richelieu. The square is lined by several bars and a hotel and at its centre is a decent fountain that the children play in during the summer months. They frolic in it. I wanted to avoid using the word 'frolic', but they do do that – what can I say? The market spills from Les Halles onto the Place du Marché, running right along its northern edge up to the steps of the church. In the summer it is full with market holders (*exposants* the French call them – they have to make everything sound seedy) and if you are late, you won't get a place because they will all be taken.

I'd started selling my beer at the market in Richelieu in February 2018 and I'd slowly increased my sales each week. Now I was making a healthy profit. It wasn't quite enough for us to live comfortably yet, but the trajectory was good.

'Bye, Albert, I love you. Be good for Mummy,' I said as I headed out of the kitchen door.

'Err, Daddy, you're a wet sandwich, Daddy.'

'Thanks, Albert.'

I said goodbye to Rose. The Tub of Thunder (that's my van, not a nickname for me) was loaded with beer. I was ready to go to market.

Burt the dog rode with me in the van. We swung into the marketplace with 1980s hair metal blaring out the window. We were late as usual. I unloaded all my paraphernalia from the van and set up some big parasols. Fred the policeman came round and took €2 for the stand.

'You're late, Monsieur Barnes,' he frowned.

I apologised and gave Fred a bottle of beer. One of the most extraordinary things I've realised here is you can fix almost anything by giving someone a bottle of beer. I sat back and remembered my life back in the rat race in London – the pointlessness was what really grated with me. Shuffling up the street in the morning and into the office reception, and there would be this fancy glass, uplit desk, and you'd walk in and think, *Who are they trying to convince this is some grand enterprise?* And the way they'd call us into meetings and talk about the work as if we were all super-motivated high achievers when 90 per cent of us didn't want to be there. Ten per cent of people thrive in offices and I have nothing but admiration for them, but the other 90 per cent of us are cannon fodder. We'd have preferred to be anywhere but in that office sitting on blue swivel chairs, trying to set up our telephone answerphones, convoluted log-ins to various malfunctioning IT systems, praying for an IT meltdown and hanging on until lunch, when we'd sortie out for an hour to shuffle around the same old sandwich shops. Then we'd squash onto a bench with three complete strangers as cars circled the three-foot patch of grass in front of us, which claimed to be a park but seemed suspiciously like a roundabout, and we were brought together in a kind of nihilistic brotherhood by our badly ironed shirts as we absently chewed our chicken-salad sandwiches, our Mars Bars, sipped our cans of San Pellegrino fizzy orange, and hoped that hour would last for ever. It doesn't.

Rose and I left London in 2016 partly because London was getting too expensive. The flats I could afford were getting smaller and smaller and so was my perspective on life. But also, partly, I was going mad. By the end I was only really focused on midweek drinking. Weekends were too busy. Crowds make me uncomfortable. Work was awful. I was a second-rate graphic designer in an office in Central London and I was deeply unhappy. It's funny − if the me that lived in London back then passed me now in the street, he'd scoff. I'm still wearing the clothes I had five years ago. My t-shirts have holes in. Jeans are covered in mud or hop sludge. I wear an old pair of trainers my dad gave me. I don't have any product in my hair. I don't particularly care how I look now. I've got more important things to worry about. It's not even that, actually. What mattered to me then seems ludicrous to me now. I didn't ever think of myself as vain back then, but I was absolutely vain. I wore clothes that I thought people would be impressed by. I cared about who made them. The me that lived in London bought matte moisturiser on more than one occasion. Shit! Matte moisturiser! Everything was for the benefit of other people. It was so painfully aspirational, but to aspire to what? That's it, isn't it? I didn't know what I was aspiring to, just that I was aspiring.

But if I passed the me from ten years ago now, I'd scoff as

well, because I didn't know what it was to live then. What a waste of time worrying about how you look is. And what a waste of time going to work and back all week just so you could get pissed on a Wednesday was.

Bloody offices. I remember when we were at school in that shitty Hertfordshire commuter town, there'd be the odd kid who came from a farm out of town and we'd laugh at them. We thought the life of an artisan was embarrassing. No, my friends and I were all going to become accountants and management consultants. Jesus Christ. What arsehole put that into our heads?

Now here I was in the market square bathing in the warm sun of central France. Yes, previously it had been the most stressful year of my life (read the first book, you tight-fisted bastards) but it was OK now. This was why we'd moved here. This was why we'd escaped the office. This was the life.

It was a searing summer at the market. Burt languished in the driver's cabin of the van, gorging on croissants fed to him by the steady stream of people visiting my stall: English friends we had met as part of the expat community out here, and French friends – our neighbours, people from the village, guys from the local football club. I'd trained a few times with the local football club, but frankly, I was so bad I'd brought shame on the English, so I'd stopped.

People coo over Burt at the market. He plays up to it. He's a shameless floozy. And the thing is, he hates these people. I know him, sitting there curled on the seat like a boa constrictor who'd swallowed a bouncy castle, giving them the glad eye.

'Does he have enough water?' they say.

'No, he only drinks the blood of virgins,' I reply under my breath. But they feed him titbits and scold me for not letting him out of the van, and I think to myself, *If you people had only studied his poo, you wouldn't be cooing over him. You'd be calling Interpol.* But you can't say that, can you? You can't ask people to study your dog's poo, and so Burt continues to win.

I chatted to everyone about anything. By that I mean I would tell anyone who would listen that the second child was easier than the first and then we'd moan about Brexit. The thing was, no one new how Brexit would play out. We were all trying to build lives over here but at any moment it felt like it could be taken away from us. Some people had applied for residency permits, but the rumour was that when it happened, they would be invalid and you'd have to apply all over again, so we sat and waited, sitting ducks, awaiting our fate. It affected Rose more than me. She fretted about how easy it would be for her family to come and see us if everyone needed a visa each time they travelled. The biggest downside of moving to France for Rose was that she couldn't see her family as much as she'd like to, and Brexit was amplifying all her fears by ten. We carried on as if there wasn't this iceberg on the horizon, but I'll tell you now, that eats away at you.

Some of my market customers would buy lots of beer. Some wouldn't buy any beer. That wasn't entirely the point. Partly the point was to sell beer, but partly the point was to talk. To be a community. Then, after the market, I'd head over to Bruno's bar, La Taverne by the Châtellerault gate, set in the walls of the town and backing onto the moat, and I'd drink an *ambrée* beer and tell unsuspecting punters that the second child was easier than the first. I'd come home with a wad of cash, which seemed like a lot, but by the time we'd paid our taxes wasn't so much, but it was OK. And so the summer rolled on.

'I love that market, Rose. It's alive. It's so *human*. Actual people buying actual products that me and my fellow traders have grown or made or in some cases bought from a giant industrial warehouse. You walk up and down that market and there are people tasting wines, sniffing cheeses, caressing aubergines in a way that only the French could, Rose. I mean, I have seen things at those vegetable stalls that wouldn't even be allowed on the internet.' Rose grimaced. I continued. 'But most of all I love the other vendors around me, Rose. That's what really makes it. We are family. Blood brothers and sisters. Even though I haven't known those guys for long, it feels like they're my oldest friends. We know everything about each other. We'd do anything for each other. Run through walls, Rose. We'd actually do that for each other.'

'You don't even know their names,' said Rose. She was jealous of my new best friends.

'Of course I know their names.'

'Well, what are they, then?'

'You want me to say their names? You actually need me to do this?' I glanced at her. It seemed she did actually need me to do this, which was a shame. 'Fine. I thought you were better than that, but OK. Well, of course, next to me there's Goat's Cheese Guy, then Sausage Woman . . .' I glanced at Rose. She wasn't buying it. '. . . Bio Cheese Woman opposite – she's like the sister I never had, Vegetable Guy, Honey Woman, Pizza Woman, Wine Guy, Olives Guy and of course, Grocery Woman.' I racked my brains for anyone I'd forgotten. 'Oh, and the other Sausage Woman down the end, but we're more just acquaintances.'

Rose had a point. I had over-egged it a little. But I did love the market. And as the summer went on, I did begin to learn their names. To my right was Antoine, who made his own goat's cheese at his farm in Marigny-Marmande, the next village after Braslou. Opposite me there was Nico, who grew ruddy-looking vegetables in Verneuil-le-Château, a village ten minutes from Braslou. The region we are in, the Touraine, is known as the garden of France because the soil round here is so fertile. Nico, despite being a small producer, always had a huge selection of beautifully grown vegetables. In summer, the sweetest tomatoes, lettuces, aubergines, fennel; in winter, all manner of squashes, beetroots and cabbages. He was maybe late twenties or early thirties, a tall, good-looking guy who flirted with his customers and consequently had queues of elderly women at his stall most weeks. I tried his technique, but my flirting comes across more as an ailing government-run counselling scheme for disgraced game-show hosts, so I settled on shouting '*Bonjour*' at startled tourists and grinning like a well-cocained tree frog. It was surprisingly successful. Every market day Nico and I would share a beer at 11 a.m. in the shadow of the church for, as he put it, *la force*.

There was Jillianne, who was normally my market neighbour. She'd spent time in Glasgow, so she would help me translate. She understood the British sense of humour. She would pass the morning eating tomatoes and laughing at my attempts to make small talk with my customers in French. She sold groceries from local producers, bread that looked like it had come from the Middle Ages, apples, potatoes, pulses, biscuits. Loads of stuff. There was Corinne, who sold organic cheese. She had the stall opposite and to the right of me, next to Nico. She was my age, although whereas I had slotted neatly into the role of village idiot, she was the mother of the group. She would want to know how you were, how your family were. She cared about everyone.

We gathered round her stall at quiet times for a coffee and to comment on whatever it might be passing by – obese dogs, a gaggle of tourists. Then there was Christine from a village called La Belle Indienne, who made small quantities of the most exquisite honey. Down the end of our row was Adrien the shepherd. He was an actual shepherd. He sold his own home-made cheese, yoghurts made from sheep's milk, and whatever else he had. At the end of the market I would swap a bottle of beer with him for some cheese. As I got to know him, he started offering me his secret stash of super-aged cheese. I don't think he knew how old it was. I suspect it had been handed down from his great-grandfather because it had achieved a state I had never seen before in cheese. Whereas the stuff he sold on his counter was milk white and fresh, this was tobacco brown and spotted with holes that looked like they had been punched out by radio-active meteorites. I swear there were fossils in it. It tasted of Roman times. There was Pascale, who would turn up in the summer to sell *saucissons* to earn extra money to pay for her family holidays. One day I noticed her writing in a little notepad. When I asked her what she was writing, she told me it was a book for her son – all the things she wished she'd known when she was young. She would give the book to her son when it was the right time. I tell you, I loved these people.

CHAPTER 2

Look, I don't mean to go on about it, I don't want you to think I'm obsessed or anything, but nothing illustrates Burt's mind better than the case of the missing dishwasher wheels. I noticed one day that one of the wheels from the bottom tray of the dishwasher had disappeared, meaning that when you pulled the tray out, if you weren't careful, it came off its runners and lurched to one side. It was OK: there were still two other wheels on that side, so it would still work as long as you were prepared. A week or so later I noticed a second wheel had come off on the same side. Now it was really unmanageable. A few days after that, the third wheel from the same side had come off. It had been rendered unusable. I knew it was Burt, not least because I noticed some chewed plastic that looked very much like it was once a dishwasher wheel in his poo. *Maybe it wasn't malicious?* you say. *Maybe he was just nervous or hungry?* Normally I would admit all of that as a possibility, but they were all from the same side, dear reader. They were all from the *same side*. If he'd taken one from one side and one from the other side, the tray would still have worked because there were still wheels on both sides. He took them all from the *same side.* It was a deliberate, calculated act of sabotage. Can't you see? He's hiding in plain sight. *But Tommy,* you say, *you're studying his poos again. We're worried about you.* Yes. No, you've got me there.

We were invited to dinner at Damien and Celia's one hot summer's night.

'*Salut*, Tom.' Damien always calls me Tom. He can't bring himself to say Tommy – it's too frivolous. It's actually a pain in the arse living opposite Damien and Celia because they're so unbelievably industrious that we're constantly looking lazy in comparison.

'*Salut*, Damien. How's it going?' I said as he held open the gate.

'Yeah, fine. Did you bring the cigars?'

'Yep.'

'Cool. You want to see my new art studio?'

'Oh, for Christ's sake, Damien,' I said under my breath. 'Yeah, sure!' I had been promising to build Rose an art studio in the barn for four years. Damien, it turned out, had knocked one up in a weekend. Not content with this, they were currently in the process of digging out and building a proper heated swimming pool in their garden. The year before, Damien had built a tower on his house. An actual tower.

French dinners, even relaxed ones like this, are quite structured. You'll have aperitifs – that might be a beer or white wine or a whisky and Coke, along with *saucisson* or *rillettes* – a sort of local pâté made with white wine or other bites to eat. Then you sit down to eat at the table and there'll be a starter – this time it was endives with vinaigrette – and then a main course – we had chicken with mushrooms, followed by cheese and dessert. I noticed early on in our move to France that French people tend to only drink one or possibly two glasses of wine with their dinner, so I try to hold back, safe in the knowledge that once dinner is finished, you could really get stuck in.

The real reason we were there was that Damien had bought an inflatable Jacuzzi, so after dinner we got in, smoked cigars and drank champagne while strong jets of bubbles blasted relentlessly at our behinds. I'm telling you, life was good.

September was hot. The school holidays finished and the market was a little less busy, but it was still a marvellous way to live, even as the evenings began to darken.

At the end of summer a kitten arrived. I assumed it was part of Rose's pregnancy cravings. Nathalie, who owns a house along from ours, had been round the week before to say they had kittens they were looking to give away, so we took one and she was the sweetest kitten you could imagine. Grey and pink fur. She had patches of fur that were a light pink. Her eyes hummed lullabies; she was the most affectionate little thing, caressing your legs in figures of eights. She just wanted to be loved. I would talk to her like you would talk to a newborn baby:

'Ah hello, my little puddy wuddy fluffy catty watty. You want a little treaty weety, silly billy?'

We called her Marple.

It was the first Friday of October. I knew it was the first Friday of October because that's how calendars work. I began my market day the same way I always did – stumbling round the house in a suffocating red-wine hangover looking for things to spread Nutella on until I came by chance across some strong coffee, which I drank, snorted and finally poured in my ears. Then I stepped outside to load the van.

'Rose. Oh my God. ROSE!'

Rose, now eight months pregnant, stuck her head out of the kitchen door. 'What?'

'Jesus Christ, Rose, there are bodies everywhere. Oh Christ. It's a massacre. Keep Albert inside.'

Rose surveyed the scene, took a sharp intake of breath and shut the kitchen door. I picked my way through the corpses laying prone across the patio. Mice and shrews were scattered around in grotesque poses. Chicks had been pulled from their nests and dismembered. In the midst of the carnage, Marple looked up at me with her lullaby eyes as she toyed with a mouse.

'Jesus, Marple. What have you done?'

Marple the cat, it turned out, was a stone-cold killer. From then on, scenes of unimaginable gore greeted us every morning. In some ways it was educational – as the summer stretched on, I got to see the entire range of rodents that lived in our neighbourhood, from the common field mice and big fat rats to rarer finds like little shrews or, best of all, *lérots*, which are sweet little mouse-like creatures with big ears and black stripes across their eyes and pompoms on their tails. Such adorable little things. All were horribly dead – splayed out on the patio in ritual killings. Nothing was safe from her razor-sharp claws. Even the dogs were scared of her. She would pummel Burt and then jump up onto the wall out of reach. I liked her. I was terrified of her, obviously, because you never knew who would be next, but I liked her. Eventually I would set her up a bed in the outbuilding where I stored my malt. She would be my protector. But I didn't have time to deal with this bloodbath now. I needed to get to the market.

Carefully picking my way round the corpses, I loaded the Tub of Thunder (again, I'm referring to my van, not myself) with beer. I noted the morning was a little fresher than usual. This year's heatwave had carried well into September, but now there was a cool wind from the east or the west or wherever these things come from. For the first time it was still dark while I loaded up. For a moment, a shadow passed across me and I shivered. 'Probably Burt's shadow,' I thought. Then I remembered that, because he was a malignant devil beast grown from one of Satan's limbs, he probably didn't have a shadow.

'Bye, Albert!' I called as Albert watched me through the living-room window.

'Er, Daddy,' said Albert, gravely, 'you're a wet bicycle poo.'

'OK, thanks, Albert.'

By the time I'd coaxed Burt onto the passenger seat of the van and rumbled out of the gates in the direction of Richelieu market, we were running late. Anxious not to lose my spot to another vendor, I put the siren and the flashing lights on (it's an old Peugeot J9 fireman's van from 1982 – a classic piece of French engineering, a sort of a giant baked bean on wheels – that I bought largely because it still had its siren) and hurtled down the Route de Richelieu at 73 kph as startled drivers pulled over to let me through, even though most of them were going faster than me.

I needn't have worried. When I arrived, there were plenty of spaces. There was an air of melancholy about the market that took me by surprise. The buzz had gone, along with several regular stallholders and about 50 per cent of the clientele. Specifically, there was a distinct lack of tourists. Normally you'd have glamorous Parisians (who everyone seemed to hate), Germans, Dutch and, most of all, British tourists marching up and down pointing at funny-shaped vegetables. Incidentally, I used to live near Baker Street in London and so I would see lots of tourists from all over the place round there and I used to scoff at how they dressed. The Italians in their brightly-coloured Puffa jackets, the French with their rucksacks and drainpipe jeans, etc. But I tell you what, now that I was over here, it was abundantly evident that it's not the Europeans who are the worst dressers. I mean, bloody hell, guys. You can spot the British from the other end of Richelieu, strutting down the Grand Rue in their North Face jackets and weird jeans plastered with brands that probably mean something to a few pricks in the wine bars of Leeds. Their over-matched accessories, the emphasis on all the wrong things, glancing about them with a veneer of defiance that fails to cover the desperation, the hours spent shuffling around a monolithic outlet centre on the outskirts of Bracknell, the fundamental lack of confidence in their appearance. Oh, Jesus.

The French, of course, with the exception of the Parisians, dress really peculiarly. Anything goes in Richelieu. You see people walking around looking like they've been fired from a circus cannon through the costume department of a West End musical and then fired back via a local garden centre. It's impossible to try and understand the way they dress. But whatever it is, they wear it much better than us – that's the point. Buried in the British psyche is the belief that when it comes to fashion, the Europeans know something that we don't and that's why, once we are out of our normal environment, we will forever walk around as if we think we

37

may have a 'kick me' sign pinned to our back. Oh, actually, the Dutch. I've just remembered the Dutch. They're much worse than us, so don't worry. They – grown adults – dress in matching clothes. I remember seeing three guys in their twenties outside the café in the square, two of them wearing dark green polo shirts and khaki shorts and the other, presumably the wild one, wearing dark green shorts and a khaki polo shirt. We're OK. It's the Dutch.

Richelieu, the lofty, elegant town with sandstone buildings perfectly uniform in their exquisite seventeenth-century architecture, brilliant white in the summer sun, had thumped back down to earth in the grey of October and now rested shabbily on the grubby cobbles of the market-place. I disembarked from the Tub of Thunder with a fundamental lack of grace, told all the vendors in turn that the second child is easier than the first, and then I set up my little table in front of the van, settled back and waited for the clients to roll up.

After an hour I'd only sold a handful of beers.

I sidled up to Jillianne, my neighbour who sold organic groceries. '*Un peu calme?*' I said.

'*Oui,*' said Jillianne. You could tell by the Gallic shrug that she wasn't surprised by it. She had fully expected it. The market was always like this in October. I hadn't even contemplated that the market was seasonal. Of course, once the summer holidays ended and the weather dampened, it would get quieter. That made perfect sense. I thought about it. *Well, I might not have the tourists to sell to, but I still have my regular customers who actually live here.* This was true. I did have lots of regulars who came each week to buy beer. So I sat back and waited for them to arrive. By 11.30 virtually no familiar faces had passed by. When I thought about it, most of my regular customers had disappeared in the last month or so.

Oh, crap, I thought. *Marple must have killed them.*

Nico the vegetable seller was still doing OK.

'It's not the season to drink beer,' he said when he had a break. He'd been watching me twiddle my thumbs.

'Nico, it's always the season to drink beer. That's the beauty of beer. Humanity will always need three things – loo roll, loo seats and beer,' I said.

'OK. Maybe in England you drink beer all year round, but round here we mostly drink beer in the summer. We drink more red wine when it gets cold.'

'Oh crap.'

This did make more sense than Marple going on some kind of rampage, but it was still a problem. When I cast my mind back, I vaguely remembered from the year previously that things had dropped off a bit in autumn, but I hadn't been doing the market then, and I'd been so busy and the brewery had been such a complete shitshow, it hadn't really registered.

'Some people still drink beer, though,' said Nico, trying to cheer me up.

But as I watched people passing by, I began to suspect there was more to it than just the season changing. The thing is, you can sell any beer to a tourist, good or bad. They don't know what it's like. They buy it once, maybe twice if they're here for a couple of weeks, and then they go home. But if you start selling bad beer to your regular customers, they will stop buying it, obviously. OBVIOUSLY. It was so bloody obvious. I mean, the tourists will buy bad beer and waddle off to wherever they came from, but the locals, no.

The truth was, my beer wasn't as good as it had been. And it wasn't ever brilliant. It had been getting progressively worse over that summer as the rising heat meant I failed to keep the fermentation temperatures in check, and yet I'd continued to peddle it out and this was the result. My core customer base – the local French people who I now realised I really depended on once the tourists had flown – had begun to desert me. Rose was due to give birth any day now and suddenly our main source of income had started drying up. I was in a bit of a bind.

CHAPTER 3

Twelfth October 2018. 'What shall we call her?' asked Rose, sitting propped up in her bed in Chinon Hospital. Chinon is an old town on the River Vienne, over-looked by a historic castle. It's also the closest town with a hospital. Rose had just given birth to our second child – a little girl who was currently snoozing in her arms.

No offence guys, but even though everyone told you how beautiful your baby was, it more than likely looked like a miniature walrus or a grizzled old vaudeville star or God knows what. They just say that stuff because it's expected, isn't it? You can't say, 'Congratulations! Your new baby looks like Bruce Forsyth.'

But our baby was already genuinely the most gorgeous little thing, with clear blue eyes like ray guns and I say that without bias.

I took a long look at her in Rose's arms and shut my eyes. This was huge. We would give her a name that would define her for the rest of her life. It had to be perfect. It had to help her navigate the world. It had to be her in name form.

Just like I did when we named our son (see book one,

you cheapskates), I slipped further and further into a deep meditative trance until finally the name came to me. It was ideal. It was a name that was written on her very soul. I took a deep breath.

'We shall call her Poitou Bobinage,' I said.

Poitou Bobinage is a business on an industrial estate between Châtellerault and Poitiers that repairs pumps. It's my favourite name for a business, so much so that I even came up with a radio jingle for them set to a jaunty radio-jingle tune:

> *If a man fixing pumps,*
> *Brings you out in goosebumps*
> *Come to Poitou Bobinage!*

I'm still plucking up the courage to turn up there with an acoustic guitar and sing it to them.

'Poitou Bobinage?' said Rose. 'What about Margot?'

'Yes, right. That's good as well. Let's go with Margot. Margot Bobinage.'

I was disappointed, but I was willing to be the bigger person.

'Just Margot,' said Rose.

'OK. Yes. That's what I said,' I mumbled.

A few days later we brought Margot home, a healthy, glowing powerhouse of a baby girl. Rose was recovering. All had gone as well as anyone could hope and so we prepared to settle back into the grind.

I knew the deal with babies now. A few sleepless nights at the start. Drink lots of coffee for a few weeks until they start sleeping properly. Don't panic and rush them to hospital when they get a cold. Just be a normal, rational adult.

Make sure they know you're in charge, and before you know it, you're on easy street. I comforted myself with the knowledge that the second one is easier than the first.

Having a child brings about many changes in one's life. For us it meant we'd really embraced wine in a box and consequently our cheap wine consumption jumped sharply. There are a few advantages to wine in a box. Firstly, it's easier to wrap than a bottle if you want to give someone the gift of wine. Secondly, generally speaking, you get better value if you buy wine in a box compared to the same amount in a bottle. Thirdly, and the most important advantage, it's much easier to hide how much you are drinking from the rest of the village. Bottles pile up quickly and you have to do the drive of shame to the bottle bank and spend hours dumping all your hundreds of bottles while people come and go, but with boxes of wine you simply throw the foil bag in the bin, recycle the cardboard and nobody will ever know you did five litres in an afternoon. If I were to give parental advice to any parents-to-be, I would say make sure you are fully stocked with box wine before your child is born. Actually, I am going to give you some parental advice. I'll start and end with all the things you should do but you inevitably won't.

Do sleep training. Let the little buggers cry. The sooner the better. Not for too long, and not if they're really losing it, but get them used to getting themselves back to sleep. Don't run in with a bottle of milk every time they cry because it will go on for ever, and the rest of your life will be shit. You won't do it, though, because you're not a monster, and when you hear your child cry it's like someone's pulling your bones out.

Don't let them stare at screens until they are eighteen. It's a drug. People say that, but I mean, when you see the effect it has on the kids, you know it to be true. Same for phones and tablets. You won't do it, though, because when you've had weeks of demands to pretend to be a dolphin or to have a 10,000th race up and down the living room on your hands and knees or to push them on a swing for an unconscionable amount of time – seriously, entire days on the swing – or to hold your legs up in the air for ages in absolute agony while they pretend you are Tower Bridge, the temptation for ten minutes or half an hour or, I don't know, four hours of your child not demanding something of you is too powerful to resist. So you will let them look at a screen.

Do what you say you will do. If you threaten to take a toy away if they throw your phone at the postman again, you'd better follow through, because if you don't, they will know you are weak. You won't do it, though, because when you haven't slept for two years and your child is battling you for absolutely everything and they've given you yet another weird virus they picked up from crèche and you are just SO UNBELIEVABLY TIRED, so tired, sooner or later you'll let something slide. And I'll tell you what you'll do then. You'll pretend you forgot you threatened to take away their favourite car if they put fish fingers in your wine glass again. You let one slide and you hope they think you just forgot as well, that your unwavering authority is still intact, but your child knows you didn't forget. Your child knows exactly what you did, and from that moment you are on the back foot and slowly your authority erodes.

Don't buy them loads of cheap plastic tat. They will use almost none of it. It will spoil them and it will litter the garden, that's all it will do. And the odd bit of tat they actually show any interest in will break instantly and cause

44

meltdowns that far outweigh any fleeting happiness they derived from said tat, and eventually all the tat will bind together in the sea and choke a 100-year-old turtle with an extended family that adores it to death. But you will buy them cheap plastic tat, because you'll be at the beach or at the zoo and other children will be being bought cheap plastic tat and they will be waving it around in the air like it's Excalibur freshly pulled from the stone, and you know your child sees it and you don't want your child not to have what other children have. So you will buy them cheap plastic tat.

Don't shout at them. Really, don't. It doesn't do any good and the moment you hear them shouting at someone else, a kid in the playground or even you, and you hear your voice in theirs and your words coming from them and, worst of all, your aggression in their voice, you'll be mortified. But you will shout at them at some point because of all the usual reasons: tiredness, desperation, and of course they can be absolute arseholes. Sometimes, when they're screaming at each other, shouting at them is the only way to be heard. But try not to do it too much. If you promise me one thing, try not to shout at them. Good luck out there.

Ninth December 2018. Margot hadn't slept. I don't mean she hadn't slept that night. I mean *Margot hadn't ever slept*. Not for more than an hour or two, anyway. Albert, our first child, now aged two and a half, was a bad sleeper, but Margot was different gravy. It had been two months of unrelenting wake-ups. And she was waking Albert up too, so it was not like one of us could get some sleep. Once they were both up, then Rose and I were both up too. Over and over again, one, two, three, four o'clock in the morning till finally Margot decided she was properly up at 5 a.m. and

45

ready to party and we'd dutifully stumble downstairs and sit on the sofa in the living room in a state of shock.

'The second one is easier than the first,' I would sob to myself as I poked around the wood burner trying to get it going again off the embers. Whereas once the sun came up Margot was a particularly jolly little baby – indeed never had I seen a creature with such a love of being alive – for Rose and me it was a horror show. It was the rack, and every day as the sleeplessness went on, we were getting stretched and stretched. Oh, she just wouldn't sleep.

I can sense I'm getting little sympathy from other parents out there. Every parent goes through it and some have it much worse than us, I know that. But for Christ's sake. Every hour, though? Is that normal? And to get her back to sleep you had to march her round the room singing hits from the musical *Oliver*. I shit you not.

We'd already made two midnight dashes to the hospital with her, both times for what turned out to be colds. It was impossible to do anything but just survive. I wasn't brewing anything. I wasn't doing anything. I was regressing back into the sea.

I don't remember much about the markets during this period. All I have are vague memories of Corinne and the gang being astounded at how tired I looked.

'The second one is easier than the first,' I'd whimper to occasional unsympathetic passers-by as they failed to buy beer.

I'm still undecided as to whether having children is a good idea. On the one hand, you get a cute baby, and on the other hand, it's a never-ending nightmare the depths of which you can't possibly imagine.

Before you have your first child, other parents will hint

about how it will change your life. You get a nod and a wink and you give them a nod and a wink back and tell yourself you're prepared for the worst. You know it's going to be difficult. You've heard it's tiring. You know you won't be able to go out like you used to. But trust me, you don't know how bad it is until it happens to you. Somewhere in your head you're still saying to yourself, *Well how bad can it be?* And the answer, it turns out, is one million out of ten. Because there's a thing that parents do to expecting couples that might be called massaging the truth but it's really just outright lying. You don't tell them about the *war*. The endless sleepless nights. The endless screaming. The endless singing. The endless jigging them to sleep. And then they wake up an hour or so later and it starts again. Oh, and the poo. And the sick. The sick! You probably should tell them, but you can't bring yourself to do it, because they are already in it now, whether they like it or not, so you say, 'It's going to be a big change!'

But this is the thing, and this is something you should tell parents-to-be: there are emotions you will experience when you have children that you simply would never experience otherwise. I mean, there's the way you feel when you're pulling shit out of their trouser leg, or wiping their vomit off your face and lips and eyes, but there are good emotions too, incomprehensibly good emotions. There's a bond you have with your children, a love that is like nothing you experience outside of this. Something so profoundly deep, bottomless and completely outside the bounds of logic. Nothing can prepare you for the sleepless nights, and equally nothing can prepare you for this love. They're a part of you, even though they are clearly not. You can feel their emotions as if they're your own. It's extraordinary.

47

And that outweighs a million sleepless nights, a million pisses on the couch, nappy changes gone wrong or crayons dragged across the walls. And if that was it, I would say of course you should have children. You'd be absolutely mad not to have children.

But then it goes on. It turns out that bond you have is a heavy burden. There's the responsibility, obviously. Looking after someone so dependent on you and someone you care so much about is hard. And you have to be careful you're not on top of them all the time. You want to tell them how to do everything, you want them to know everything that you didn't know, but you're being overbearing again, Tommy! You've got to step back. But that's not the worst bit.

There's something terrible that you become aware of, that lurks on your shoulder – the thought of your children being unhappy. People don't tell you how hard that is to deal with. And I'm talking about just the *thought* of it. Our children are still young and nothing very bad has happened to them. Hopefully it won't, but who knows? But the thought of it is enough to empty me. I try not to think about it, but sometimes I can't help myself and when I do, I want to die. I'm not being glib. I think about them being lonely or unhappy and for a moment, I can't cope with it. The other day Albert came to me and said he was all alone in the playground at school and I'm telling you I crumpled inside. And I was furious and upset all together, and I wanted to shout at other parents and teachers and children until gradually I calmed down and I had to accept that that's life. Sometimes kids are going to be all alone. We can try and help our children make friends, we can try and build their confidence, but you're being overbearing again, Tommy! We can't control it all for them. The more you try and control it all, the worse you make it. They have to do it themselves and they will be lonely and that kills me, I'm telling you. All you can do is try to switch it off, but every now and then the thought of it pops into your mind and it feels like the end of the world.

I don't know if other parents feel like that – maybe I drank too much gin as a child – but I can barely cope with it, and from a purely selfish point of view, sometimes I wonder if it would be better to have not had kids in the first place. But, you know, I wake up in the morning and Albert coming down the stairs and Margot waking in her cot is the highlight of my day. I can't wait to see them and just to see them gives me joy that I never knew existed before we had children. And then, as every parent knows, the day goes rapidly downhill from there.

'Hi, Fred, how's it going?'

'It's going,' said Fred. Fred doesn't talk much – and not just because I'm around. I've seen him in the company of other people. He doesn't talk much. When he has something to say, he says it. It takes a bit of getting used to, but I like that about Fred. I'm the sort of twat that has to fill the gaps in conversation – I don't have the confidence to be happy sitting there in silence – but with Fred as my teacher, I am learning. I went into his kitchen and put a couple of beers on the table and Fred got an unlabelled bottle of fizz out of the fridge.

'It's an old one.' he said. He doesn't ask if you want a glass of fizz – it's obligatory.

Fred lives up on the hill behind Braslou with his wife Karinne and their three daughters. He is a farmer and *vign-eron*: that is to say, he makes wine. There aren't that many winemakers around Braslou, as we're a little bit away from Chinon, where most of the local wine is made, but there are the Plouzeaus, who make some really super organic wine that we can't afford up on the hill in Razines next to Braslou, and there's Annabelle Chesseron, who makes a red Chinon with Cabernet Franc, a super Touraine white wine with Sauvignon blanc called l'Usufruit and a Blanc de Blancs fizz with Chardonnay, so we're doing all right. She's on the way to Île-Bouchard. But Fred is my favourite, and not just because he's in Braslou. Winemaking isn't his main income, I don't think; I think he may earn more from the farming. His winemaking to me seems more like a public service. He makes a really great sparkling wine and a red made from Cabernet Franc grapes that he grows behind his house. He's a small producer – he makes it all in a little tumbledown outbuilding at the end of his garden – and he sells mostly to the local hunt clubs and village associations. His wines are very reasonably priced. He sells big ten-litre boxes of red wine at €15 a pop and bottles of sparkling wine at €4,50. The red's supposed to be a table wine – a wine you drink in between snazzy wines, but it's better than lots of reds I've tasted that cost four times that. The thing about Fred is he used to work in one of the top vineyards in Chinon, you see. Fred knows how to make wine.

After we've tasted from several unmarked bottles – fizz, red wine, white wine, something they call *pine*, which is a mix of *eau de vie* and wines and fruit juices – we move on to my beer. On this particular day I was there nominally to pick up some of Fred's fizz for the Christmas period. Really I was there for something else.

'If I'm honest, Fred, I've been having a lot of trouble at

the brewery. The beer has been fermenting at too high a temperature. Because the beer is no good, I think my main core of clients has deserted me. We've got a newborn child who we have to feed, and she barely sleeps at all. We're all so tired and I just don't know what I'm going to do,' I said.

Fred nodded sagely, reached into the fridge and got out another bottle of fizz. You see, Fred can't understand a word I'm saying. I mean, if I repeat myself, if I try and find several different ways of saying what I'm trying to say, then he gets it. But if I just waffle on with my terrible French, making up words that I think sound French as I go, Fred's got no idea what I'm talking about and after a hard day in the fields or the vines he doesn't have the energy to try and find out. He just gives me fizz and hopes I'll stop talking. After going round his house to buy wine for a couple of years, I realised he's the perfect counsellor.

I'd been looking for someone to talk to for a while now. I mean, I should talk to my wife, and I do sometimes, but when it's stuff like this – when it's things that directly affect the family – I can't bring myself to tell Rose how bad it is because I'm the one who's been charged with providing for the family and I find it too embarrassing to admit I'm failing. I need to solve the problems myself.

I tried confiding in Gadget the grumpy miniature horse once or twice. I'd go out to the orchard in the evening and breathe into his nostrils and then we'd chat. It would seem like he understood my pain for a little while, but then he'd bite my kneecap and I realised he didn't care about what I was saying at all. He'd just spent ten minutes waiting for the right moment to bite my kneecap. I even tried talking to Burt the dog, but I got the distinct impression he was deriving a great deal of pleasure from my misery. So when

51

I realised I could waffle at Fred and there would be no judgement, no advice that I knew I was too proud to follow, no hard truths to face up to, because he hadn't understood anything I'd said, it was a great relief. I'd roll out of Fred's kitchen high on fizz and with a renewed vigour.

By the end of November the beer had all but stopped selling. The money we'd made in the summer had seen us through so far, but it was starting to dwindle.

We alternate Christmases with our families, me and Rose. This year we were due to spend Christmas with Rose's family. Since we'd moved to France, Rose missed her sisters terribly, so Christmas was a huge deal. The problem was, her sisters and their husbands were successful and well off. They'd decided to rent a house in Italy for Christmas. I should have told Rose that we would be bankrupted if we travelled all the way to Italy and stayed in this house; I mean, the petrol alone, and we'd have to stay in hotels on the way there and on the way back, and the house itself cost a fortune, but I was too proud and stupid and I just couldn't do it. However, all was not lost. Now it was almost December and the Christmas markets were about to begin, and so I signed up for a market every weekend till just before Christmas. I felt sure this was our big chance to claw some money back. Maybe even enough to get us to Italy.

French Christmases are less present-orientated. France at Christmas is all about the family and the meal on Christmas Eve. As Christmas starts to draw closer, supermarket shelves start to fill up with tins of foie gras, caviar, champagne and ginormous boxes of chocolates. At the market the fish stalls overflow with oysters and lobsters. They're not so interested in turkey and all that, but you can find them if you look hard enough. My overriding memory of our first Christmas in France was hacking off the head of a huge turkey on the dining-room table with a blunt knife on Christmas morning while Rose's mum looked on aghast. If you get them from the local farms, they leave the heads on them. You have to pull all the innards out as well.

Most towns in France have a Christmas market now, but the thing about Christmas markets is you get the feeling they're not very French. More specifically, the idea of the Christmas market that's been sold across Europe looks to me to be decidedly German, and consequently the French treat it with a degree of suspicion. But they try their best to embrace it as we do, because with hot wine and ready-wrapped last-minute Christmas presents, it does seem like a decent idea, doesn't it?

The Christmas market at Richelieu was the first up at the beginning of December. I had high hopes. It was a big market – well organised. It was expensive to get a stall, more than €100, but I planned on a making ten times that amount.

A fine Christmas tree was resident in the middle of the market square where the fountain normally is when I arrived to start setting up my stall. Around it maybe twenty neat white canvas booths had been erected for the vendors. Father Christmas patrolled the market looking for children to confuse. Other, more tenuous costumed characters roamed as well. A few stalls along a group of large, jolly Germans from Schaafheim, a town twinned with Richelieu, had set up their stall selling mulled wine, crêpes and a light, pure, perfectly balanced German lager with a lovely hoppy finish. I can't remember the name of it – which is the classic sign of a good beer – but you taste beers like that and you realise you still have an awful long way to go.

There were stalls selling jewellery. Handbags. Antoine the goat's-cheese man had a stall there. A guy was roasting chestnuts. The forbidden smell of fried doughnuts drifted across from a stall, which also sold churros and candyfloss (*barbe à papa* in French – Dad's beard!). So many stalls. So many interesting things. Fireworks were being readied in Richelieu park behind the square for Sunday night for the big finale. The excitement among the stallholders was palpable.

And then no one turned up. I'm exaggerating. Almost no one turned up. Pretty much no one turned up. Virtually no one turned up. It was a catastrophe. I don't blame them. I wouldn't have either. From the moment the market opened it began pouring with rain. Winter rain – ice cold, saturating and relentless. But that wasn't the only reason. You see, the *gilets jaunes* had just come on the scene.

The *gilets jaunes* are a peculiarly French protest movement. Admirable in so many ways, but ultimately mad as an ostrich doing the can-can in a space suit. From what I can understand, the *gilets jaunes* movement started because the French president, Macron, was trying to raise taxes on diesel-powered cars and a lot of the French had had enough, because if you're not in a city you depend on your car for a living. Besides, most French cars are diesel because for years the authorities had been saying that diesel was best. So, particularly for the people who didn't live in the big cities and therefore depended more on cars to get around, hiking the price of diesel after telling everyone to get diesel cars was a killer. More than this, there was a general feeling that for the everyday citizen, their standard of living was being eroded while an elite got richer and richer. Well, they're right, aren't they? That's exactly what's happening all over the world. And unlike the British, whose solution, absurdly, was to vote for Brexit, the French (because they are bloody brilliant) actually decided to do something positive about it. They organised themselves into the *gilets jaunes* movement – so called because they all wore the fluorescent-yellow jackets that under French law you're required to carry in your car at all times in case of a breakdown – and they went out and protested. They blocked traffic. They held open the barriers at motorway toll booths so people could travel for free. They demonstrated in big cities. They took on the authorities and, despite some pretty brutal battles with the police, they didn't back down until eventually Macron was forced to concede. He dropped his planned fuel-tax increases.

But by now the *gilets jaunes* were on a roll. It wasn't just this particular tax increase, you see, it was everything. All the little taxes, all the benefits being cut. Pensions getting smaller. The age of retirement going up. Longer working hours. All this stuff, and they were absolutely right again. This isn't what we were promised. With the wealth there is in the world and the technology we now have, it isn't fair that we should have to work longer and have less money because 0.001 per cent of the world want another gold-plated bidet for their Learjet.

The *gilets jaunes* are really flying now, but this is where it starts getting classically French. A guy from the *gilets jaunes* starts to negotiate with the government. Brilliant – you've forced the government to negotiate. You're winning. Except other members of the *gilets jaunes* claim that the whole point of the collective is that there isn't one leader who speaks for them. They disown the guy who's negotiating. Other rival *gilets jaunes* stand up and claim to be spokespeople and get shot down in a sort of negative Spartacus moment. They start threatening each other with death. They're sending their own people actual death threats. Different branches of the *gilets jaunes* emerge – the People's Front of *gilets jaunes* and the *gilets jaunes* Front of Judea, etc. That's not enough shittery. Suddenly, and this is where it gets brilliant, other rival *gilets* movements spring up. The *gilets blancs*! And even better the *foulards rouges* – the red scarves – a counter movement against the *gilets jaunes* who seem to be saying 'yeah, you're probably right about all the taxes and standard-of-living stuff but you're blocking me from getting to my yoga class, so I'm not having it'. But then the *foulards rouges* start splitting into factions, of course they do, and some of the *foulards rouges* join the *gilets jaunes* in condemning other *foulards rouges*. I don't know what the *gilets blancs* are doing at this point. Probably hand-to-hand combat with the purple G-strings. The French just don't know when to stop arguing, and eventually it becomes counterproductive. Gradually sympathy for the movement among the general public began to erode because no one could understand what was going on any more.

There's more to it than this, of course. The far right tried to appropriate the movement for its own ends, as it always does. So did the far left. It got pretty nasty. But in its purest form it was just disgruntled everyday people, and I tell you what, before it ate itself up, they did force Macron into making billions of pounds of concessions and you have to respect that.

One of the *gilets jaunes'* main achievements in 2018 was to destroy the Christmas retail economy by putting on large-scale, sometimes violent demonstrations in towns and cities and therefore putting shoppers off venturing out. Consequently, back at Richelieu market, in the Arctic rain, nobody was going to turn up in case they got caught up in a riot. It's estimated they cost the economy €2 billion that Christmas. By my calculations about a billion of that was mine. It was not a successful weekend in many other respects. Just when I thought I'd reached the nadir, the sun dipped behind the grand buildings in the Place du Marché and I realised that the little white stands we were in didn't have any lighting in them. At this point every other stall-holder switched the lights on that they'd brought with them because, of course, you needed to bring your own lights, while I sat there in the dark as the rainwater ran through the cobbles and pooled around my feet. After two days of this, I packed the van up with soggy boxes of beer, several of which burst through the wet cardboard and smashed on the floor, and an empty cash box and headed back up the road to Braslou.

I chalked the Richelieu market disaster down to bad luck, but at this point both the rain and the *gilets jaunes* showed no sign of abating. I was concerned.

The following weekend was the Christmas market at Azay-le-Rideau. Azay-le-Rideau is the real deal. Whereas Richelieu is a little way off the tourist route, Azay-le-Rideau is firmly on the tourist trail.

Richelieu is a town built on a grid – straight roads and right-angle turns – but Azay-le-Rideau is a much older town sunk into a valley on the way to Tours composed of narrow lanes that snake around an enormous Renaissance château by the River Indre. It has a funny history. I mean, not funny ha-ha – it was burned to the ground in the fif-teenth century by a retreating army loyal to Charles VII after the inhabitants started taking the piss out of him from the walls of the town. The French, like much of mainland Europe, are still learning to laugh at themselves. Anyway,

Azay-le-Rideau was a town with a genuine tourist pedigree. Surely the market would pay dividends. I revved up the Tub of Thunder (the van, not me) that Saturday morning in the freezing, pouring rain and set off in the dark. It's about a forty-five-minute drive from Braslou. There was hardly anyone on the road save for the ubiquitous tradesmen pissing in lay-bys that you always see in France, but occasionally I'd pass cars tiptoeing along that would flash me furiously. I waved back merrily and continued on. When I got to the market there were almost no other vendors there. I found out later there'd been warnings on the radio all morning telling people not to travel because due to the particular combination of freezing temperatures and heavy rain the roads had turned completely to black ice. I'd happily rolled there in a forty-year-old van with its original tyres, little realising that my life was on the line.

And for what? It was supposed to be an all-day affair but by 11.30 a.m., once again nobody had turned up. Indeed, even the few other stallholders that had braved the ice had left. The only people there were me and a local *vigneron* opposite. We exchanged booze, marvelled when our only customers of the morning – an intrepid bus of OAPs from the local retirement home – turned up and skated around in a state of extreme confusion before being shepherded back onto their bus like curling stones, and then we packed up and I made the treacherous forty-five-minute trip home as the back end of the van slid from left to right on every turn.

Still Margot didn't sleep.

The following weekend was the last of my Christmas markets, in Les Ormes. By now I'd all but given up. Les Ormes is a town over towards Descartes (birthplace of the philosopher René Descartes), about thirty minutes east of

Braslou, through verdant hills and empty sandstone villages. It wasn't a big market, but I got the sense the people there cherished it. It was set in cavernous stables opposite the château (there are about as many châteaux round here as there are Pret a Mangers in London), which helped because it was under cover. I turned up with several kegs and my beer pump, expecting the worst. The best way to sell beer is direct, you see. If I could put the beer in kegs and sell it myself for €2 a glass, that meant I wasn't paying for bottles or labels, and the process of getting it into kegs was much quicker. If no one turned up however, it was a moot point. I went into the stables and was assigned a little stall with a metal frame around it and a large table to set out my beer on. All around me people were putting up fairy lights around their stands. People were smiling and singing and I felt like I'd entered an alternative universe. It was as if I was in a video shoot for a Mariah Carey Christmas single. Hadn't they heard about the *gilets jaunes*? Hadn't they seen the weather outside? The market was well organised and jolly, which I found excruciating, because I was waiting in horror to see these poor innocent people's faces when they opened the doors and no one came in, but, to my shock, as soon as they opened the doors, people flooded in. The whole town came out to support it. Families strolled through the stables drinking beer and eating crêpes and buying presents. Over the course of the weekend I sold everything I had. It was a Christmas miracle.

And so we drove to Italy for a week to spend Christmas with Rose's family. If you think the French are crap drivers, wait until you see these guys. I mean, as a stuffy British driver, your first feeling when you see the Italians drive is outrage.

They are not playing by the rules, guys, and the one thing that really gets us Brits steamed up is people who don't play by the rules. But as it goes on, you start to understand it. It's not that they're not playing by the rules, well not quite, anyway. They're playing a different game. And the object of their game isn't to follow the rules: it's to not get caught not following the rules and if you don't get caught then people applaud you. Once you get it, then it's sort of OK again. Indeed, you start to marvel at the way they operate.

We got stuck in a traffic jam on the hot, dusty motorway outside of Rome and we were immediately impressed by the way some drivers used the hard shoulder. If the traffic started to move it meant little gaps appearing between cars as people accelerated. A surprisingly large number of drivers saw this as an opportunity. As the cars started to move, people would zip onto the hard shoulder, whizz past three or four cars and then pull into one of the tiny gaps that had opened up before everything came to a stop again, thus jumping their way along the queue. Then at one point we all pulled to the side as an ambulance flashed its way through the traffic jam. Close behind it was a police car. Close behind that was what might have been an unmarked police car. I'll give them the benefit of the doubt. Close behind that, slipstreaming it, in fact, was a little clapped-out yellow Fiat from the 1980s that definitely wasn't a police car. I watched as the Fiat trailed the emergency services all the way into the distance, shedding rust as it chuntered along merrily past the static traffic, and something clicked in my mind.

As you go further south you get closer to death. People live in a less prescriptive way. They live more on their instincts; they act on their desires. It felt to me that in Italy they live a more authentically human existence, and once my outrage had subsided I was jealous of them. The truth was, I wanted to be that guy in the clapped-out yellow Fiat. I vowed to take this Italian mentality back with me to Braslou.

In Italy, when it comes to driving, no one plays by the rules, whereas in the UK everyone plays by the rules. In France, people try and play by the rules, but the thing is, the rules in France are absolutely insane, so it ends up being a different kind of chaos, a classically French chaos. Because in France there are two completely contradictory traffic systems that operate at the same time. *Um . . . What did you just say, Tommy?* OK, reader, take a deep breath. This is not going to be easy for you. You see, there's the normal traffic system that is good and proper, where our actions on the road are governed by signs and road markings and life makes sense, and then there's *priorité à droite* – an alternative world where lines do not exist and you need to know only that you must cede to the person on your right. This classic French shitshow is at its most magnificently absurd when it comes to roundabouts. The problem is this: normally, if you're at a roundabout in France, you give way to the person on the *left* (because in France you drive on the right). However, if there is no dotted line across your road as you enter the round-about, for instance, the law of *priorité à droite* applies. Instead of giving way to the left, you have to give way to the *right*.

So, Tommy, you're telling me that at some roundabouts you give way to the left and at some you give way to the right? But that doesn't make sense. Why wouldn't they just have one system that is the same across all of France? Tell me, Tommy. TELL ME WHY FOR GOD'S SAKE! Let go of my shoulders, dear reader, and calm yourself. The French cannot agree on which system to use and the French being the French, nobody will back down from the argument. *Priorité à droite* is the old system. It made sense when cars were slower and there were fewer on the roads and there were no road markings. Its great advantage is that it's an extremely simple system to remember. It has two minor disadvantages: firstly, it causes lots of accidents. You could be driving at sixty miles per hour on a long straight road and a car can pull out right in front of you and you have to slam on the brakes and let them in. It's terrifying. But if that was the only system, then, I don't know, maybe you'd adapt. The second minor disadavantage, and in the interests of fairness it must be said that this would apply to pretty much any system, is that if you then add an entirely contradictory system, it causes sheer, bollocking chaos.

But this is insane, Tommy. Why can't they just adopt one system across the whole of France? Can't you make them adopt one system? IN THE NAME OF GOD, TOMMY, MAKE THEM ADOPT THE ONE SYSTEM. Take your hands from my neck, please.

Now, dear reader, I need you to brace yourself, because this is going to drive you nuts. There are towns in France that have both systems operating at once. Two completely contradictory systems operating simultaneously. SIT BACK DOWN, DEAR READER. Sit the hell down. Because this will blow your shitting mind, I shit you not. There's a roundabout in Saint-Gervais-les-Trois-Clochers that operates a *priorité à droite* no-road-markings system *except* for one entry that has a white line and a stop sign. What the shit? This is so confusing. You're giving way to the right at all the entries to the roundabout except for one entry that has a stop sign and an unbroken white line across it. Why do you have to stop here? Which way are you supposed to give way to? Both ways? Can you ever enter the roundabout? There's something distinctly quantum physics about this roundabout in Saint-Gervais. I try not to ever enter the roundabout from the road with the stop sign for fear of both existing and not existing at the same time. I just feel like that would do something to my bowels.

Now, just settle down again, dear reader. Try and grip something as tightly as you can. In Chaveignes, the village on the edge of Richelieu, they built a new round-about by the supermarket, and when they first built it, they had road markings on two of the entry points – the two opposite each other – and no road markings at the two entries perpendicular to them. This meant that you could be entering the roundabout on the road with the markings giving way to the left while the guy to your left is entering on the road without markings and there-fore giving way to the right. You're both giving way to each other! I shit you not, it created some kind of tear in the fabric of space and time. There were people there for years, dear reader. People grew old at that round-about waiting for each other to go. Whole generations of families came and went at that roundabout. They fixed it eventually because the *gendarmes* couldn't cope with the surge in missing-persons reports. Now it's marked up like a normal roundabout in a normal world and people can return to their families.

The start of 2019 was hard, but we scraped along. Little trickles of beer sold at the farm shop. I sold bits here and there. Bruno, the café owner in Braslou, started buying small quantities. January and February were bleak, desperate, but we hung tight, loading the wood burner up with oak and taking brisk walks through the forests with Damien and Celia, while all around large, organised hunts took place. Damien had been on these hunts when he was younger. He could interpret the various trumpet noises that came from deep within the thickets – some meant they'd caught a deer, but I suspect most meant it was time for another drink – either way, Damien knew what was happening in the hunt, so we felt fairly safe.

We ate stews – boeuf bourguignon or pork and mustard stew with Normandy cider and crème fraîche. I'll tell you my boeuf bourguignon recipe. It's quite like other boeuf bourguignon recipes, but with a couple of fundamental differences.

Ingredients

- Some butter
- A bag of little onions
- A carton of mushrooms
- Lardons. Lardons are fatty little bacon bits
- 1 or 2 cloves of garlic
- 1 large onion (chopped)
- 1 kilo of beef chopped into fist-sized chunks and dusted in seasoned flour. The best is Charolais beef. Interesting aside: Charolais cows are yellow and are 90 per cent buttock (at a guess)
- A ten-litre box of Fred's red wine. Most recipes call for a bottle of Burgundy wine, but my recipe calls for a ten-litre box of Fred's red because it takes a long time to cook boeuf bourguignon – you need

to start cooking it in the morning – so one bottle simply wouldn't keep you on your game.

- Some stock. Any will do really, but beef stock is best
- A bay leaf
- A comfortable chair with armrests that will balance a glass (IMPORTANT)

Method

It's 11 a.m. Firstly, open the box of Fred's red and pour yourself a memorable quantity of wine. If you want, I'll tell you the rest of the recipe, but to be honest, anything after this is strictly optional.

OK, if we must. Fry the small onions and mushrooms in a knob of butter the size of an armadillo's heart. Often recipes call for a mixture of butter and olive oil, but I'm firmly of the belief that butter keeps you young, so I say stick to butter. Once you've browned the mushrooms and little onions, scoop them out and put them aside. This is where I begin to diverge from the classics. Most recipes call for you to return the browned mini onions and mushrooms half an hour before the end of the cook, but for my recipe, and this is quite an important step, you must find them congealed in the bowl you left them in the next day, because you were so pished you forgot to put them back in.

More wine for you, my friend. Fry the lardons, garlic and the chopped onion. Now children come in and out of the kitchen demanding, crying. Partners will appear and disappear, disapproving, angry. Things will catch fire. More wine, please. Soon all these distractions will whirl to the periphery and you will be alone with your stew. Brown off the huge chunks of fatty beef. Pour in a litre of Fred's red. Then pour a litre in to the stew (snarf!). Let it boil down a bit. Chuck in some stock and the bay leaf. Now sit on your comfortable seat and place your wine on the armrest. Bask in the warmth of the majestic Fred's red.

Stir the stew once in a while, if you can still feel your legs. Set an alarm for the evening some time. It doesn't need to be this particular evening. It will be ready when the sauce has cooked down and the meat is soft and pulls apart. It matters not. You are an emperor and you rule your peaceful kingdom from upon a cloud.

By March 2019 the people of the Pays de Richelieu were emerging from hibernation and starting to return to Richelieu market, and I knew that if I could just keep going until the Braslou Marché de l'Asperge – the asparagus festival – on the second Sunday of May, I would be back in the game. The Marché de l'Asperge is my home festival, and the glorious Braslousians love beer almost as much as they love asparagus. And they love asparagus.

From March onwards every other field around here is lined with strips of plastic sheets about a metre wide that span from one end of the field to the other. It's all white asparagus. They absolutely go shit for tits for it here. It's an obsession. Neighbours turn up offering you carrier bags full of the stuff.

You need to know what you're doing with white asparagus. It can be woody and inedible. You need to get fresh asparagus and peel it from the head up to the end. I don't know why you have to do it in that direction, but someone who knows what they're talking about told us that. I think it was Marie Richard, Monsieur Richard's wife. I believe the thinner ones are more sought after, but I am prepared to be corrected. Alexis, a farmer in Razines, tells me the real factor is the ground it's grown in. You have to cut it some way up the stem and then you boil it for fifteen or twenty minutes and serve it with a mustard vinaigrette, and if it's cooked well, it's delicious – juicy, fragrant, much, much better than that green asparagus guff. As I say, they go shit for tits for white asparagus in the Pays de Richelieu. The season is short, April, May, maybe June, but the thing about asparagus is you harvest it and it grows again straight away, so you get loads and loads of crops in those few months. That's why the place goes mental, because everyone is trying to grow as much asparagus as they can in two months and the festival in Braslou is a celebration of this.

A few of the big dogs come down to the festival to show off their asparagus – tables and tables of the stuff in plastic trays or bundles tied with rubber bands. The rest of us get drinking and eating and that's it. Annabelle, who has the vineyard on the way to Île-Bouchard, has a wine stall opposite where I set up. Sometimes Fred is there selling his fizz. Aside from me there are two other *buvettes* (drinks tents), and the Milcent bar and restaurant run by Bruno and Françoise does a good trade. It's a congenial atmosphere. It's Braslou all over – no farting about, just the good bits.

Finally it was the second Sunday of May and the Fête de l'Asperge was upon us. I called round to Damien's at 6 a.m. as planned. Damien always helps me man the stall at the Marché de l'Asperge.

'I stopped drinking at two a.m. because I knew we had the market today,' said Damien.

'Thanks, Big D. Are you OK?' I'd started calling Damien 'Big D', much to his total indifference.

'I've sprained my ankle. I can't really walk. Anyway, let's get the van loaded up.' The guy was unbelievable.

By ten o'clock the market had exploded into an orgy of mild-mannered people walking up and down the street buying asparagus and drinking beer. We ploughed through the kegs. It was our third year there and it felt like we had become a feature of the market now. People came to seek us out. Old friends turned up. We saw Ali and David there. When we first moved out there, we used to spend a lot of time with Ali and David, an English couple who live in Richelieu who took us under their wing, but gradually we lost touch with them. I loved those guys, but when we had Albert we didn't see anyone much for a year and we never really got our friendship back on track.

'Guys, we should meet up. We haven't seen you in ages,' I said.

'Definitely. We'll do lunch. We'll organise a barbecue,' they said. We wouldn't meet up.

A man who in my head was wearing a black roll-neck but might not have been tapped me on the shoulder while I was pouring beers. He was suave. He had brilliant white hair, was tanned, probably in his sixties, but had clearly embraced moisturiser. He could have been straight from a 1960s secret-agent film.

'I'm Patrick. I'm a wine distributor. I'm looking for a beer to start distributing as well. I like your story. Here's my card. Give me a ring.' He handed me his card.

'Great, thanks, Patrick. Here, have a beer,' I said.

'No thanks, it's a bit early for me,' he said.

'Ah, got you.' He needed to keep a clear head for that

afternoon's assassination of the head of a global criminal empire who'd set up an elaborate base in a dormant volcano. Patrick melted back into the crowd.

It was immediately clear that this was the work of a professional. This wasn't some clown who'd stumbled upon an opportunity: no, this was meticulously planned – days, weeks in the making. The low-value stuff was left intact, but the high-value stuff – the hummus, the goat's cheese, the *poire tapée*, the olives – had been systematically eaten from upon the coffee table in the living room.

'BURT, YOU COMPLETE SHIT! YOU ENEMY OF THE PEOPLE!' When I came down from putting Margot to bed, Burt was smirking around in the kitchen and I knew immediately he'd done something. Then when I saw the ruins of the spread on the coffee table, I knew exactly what was going on. It had been a shit of a day. I'd spent half an hour that morning trying to negotiate the roundabout in Chaveignes. The kids had behaved like monsters all day and it had taken the skills of a veteran FBI hostage negotiator to eventually get them to bed. The only thing keeping me from throwing myself out of the window was the thought of a delicious local goat's cheese and some *poire tapée*.

Poire tapée is one of my favourite local delicacies. It comes predominantly from a village called Rivarennes up towards Azay-le-Rideau, and it's a whole pear that's been flattened and dried in order to preserve it. To bring it back to life they put it in a jar of syrup and white wine. I first had it when I was selling beer at an open day at the vineyard La Domaine des Quatre Vents in Cravant-les-Côteaux. The owners of the vineyard have an open day every summer where they set up giant barbecues at the entrance to the vineyard. They light them all in the morning and there's a white smoke that drifts across the courtyard as we set up, bringing a wonderful smell, because instead of using charcoal for the barbecues, they use chopped-up old vines. They invite local producers to come and set up stalls around the vineyard, so I ended up there with a cheese producer, a honey producer, and there was a *poire tapée* producer selling there as well. At lunchtime we sat in the shade and shared our food on a long table. After the barbecue, the *poire tapée* man came and put a *poire tapée* in each of our wine glasses and topped it up with some syrup from the jar. You pick the *poire tapée* out and eat it whole; it explodes in your mouth because as it's rehydrated, it's taken in all the wine and syrup, and it's sensational. Then you drink the syrup that remains in your glass and you hope the *poire tapée* guy will come back and give you another one. It's one of those local delicacies that you think should be known right across the world. And then you have a good stare at it and you realise why it's not. The *poire tapée,* once it's been dried out and then rehydrated with wine and syrup and is suspended in the jar, looks exactly, down to the last wrinkle, like an old man's testicle. I could see that might put some people off.

I wandered around the coffee table in the lounge wondering how I could have been that stupid. I remembered now, Burt watching with interest as I unpacked the shopping a few days previously. He was noting down the high-value goods. His terrible mind was already plotting – working out timings, fences, possible alibis. And this was the result. An entire table's worth of snacks lost to that despicable creature. I'd been yearning for a night in with the *poire tapée* especially, and that bloody dog, that furry balloon of noxious gas had eaten it all. The thing was, Burt would throw the *poire tapée* up later. That wasn't the point. The point was I couldn't eat it. That was his motivation. Of course, I couldn't prove anything yet. God, I couldn't wait to study his poo.

It got hot, and hot means beer sales. Suddenly summer was here. Beer sales rocketed. I could barely keep up with demand. I was getting phone calls every day from new people wanting beer. Tourists turning up at the brewery at all hours. The market at Richelieu was busier than ever. I would sell hundreds of euros worth of beer there. The problem I had was I hadn't worked hard enough in the winter to build up my stock, and now I didn't have enough time to brew because I was so busy selling. Stocks were depleting. There were fêtes every other weekend. Port-de-Piles, Azay-le-Rideau, Faye-la-Vineuse. Oh, and the Fête des Jeunes Agriculteurs – the young farmers' fair.

Jesus Christ, the Fête des Jeunes Agriculteurs. I knew it was quite a big deal. It's a region-wide fair that is held in a different place each year. This year it was taking place just outside of Chinon, which is my manor, so I was invited to have a stall. I rolled in aboard the Tub of Thunder (the van, etc.) with four kegs of Berger Blonde and a couple of IPA, and from the moment I arrived at 8 a.m. things exploded like a DIY gas-boiler installation. These men and women, the growers of produce, the keepers of livestock, know how to *fête*.

There was a racetrack marked out with straw bales in the middle of the fairground. Initially I wasn't sure why. A line of the most enormous tractors stretched for a kilometre along one side of the field. People walked up and down regarding them as if they were in an art gallery. There were strange stalls. I'd done a few markets now, so I tended to recognise a lot of my fellow stallholders, but here there were quite a few I'd never seen before. There was a man selling home-made cheese boards for extraordinary amounts of money. I watched him trying to sweet talk passers-by, but you'd have to be mad to buy something like that. There was just no way he was going to sell a thing.

From the get-go, parades of merry, drunk farmers on ancient farm vehicles circled the field in a procession. Groups of men and women hit the bars immediately. Then the races began. Combine-harvester races. Hulking battle-ready machines painted in lurid colours, adorned with skulls and crossbones or, conversely, cuddly toys, which powered round the dirt track crashing into each other as the crowds roared them on. It was fantastic. And everyone was drinking. I was ploughing through the kegs.

What was interesting was that I got a taste of what it's like on the other side of the bar. Most of my life I had been the twat getting drunk, but now I was the bartender and I realised that most drunk people are fine, but there's always one or two who are total cocks. I'm a good drunk generally. I might make a tit out of myself, but if anyone suffers, it's me, and I enjoy life when I'm drunk. Most people are like that. But there are some people who turn. You all know them. There's normally one in the group, and they might be a nice guy in the everyday world, but when they drink, something comes over them, an alter ego, and they switch in an instant to mean and pitiless. If this is you, then stop drinking, because everyone, especially your friends, think you're an arsehole when you're like that.

A group of six or seven middle-aged men, local farmers and *vignerons*, arrived at my stand about 1 p.m. They all seemed like friendly guys, apart from one of the younger men, who I immediately got a bad feeling about. He was drunk already, which normally I would find impressive, but this was different. You learn quickly at these things. The first mistake I made was to give them a free beer. I'd changed the keg and had poured a beer to make sure it was working OK, so when they turned up I offered them this beer free. It was an act of kindness but, when you're an arsehole, an act of kindness is a sign of weakness. From then on, this guy was saying things like, 'It's time for the barman to buy a round.' He'd only say it when his friends weren't in earshot; he was a coward. It was hard to keep count of the drinks because they would order a lot and then other people would arrive and they would chat and order more drinks and pay. They would always pay, but it might be a little while after they'd ordered. But when it came to this guy's round, he claimed he had paid when he hadn't. He knew he hadn't paid – he was smirking like a prick, but the second mistake I'd made was not writing down the drinks that hadn't been settled, so I couldn't be sure. We had an argument. He was hammered now. His friends wanted to pay for him, but he refused and I didn't want to take money from them. I'm not brilliant at conflict. Eventually I backed down, as I have done in these situations throughout my life, and another little notch was whittled off my self-esteem. He had his drinks for free and deep down somewhere I felt a familiar tingling of humiliation. They'd bought so much beer it wasn't a big deal, but God, I wish I'd hit him on the head with a large spanner.

I wonder what people get out of that. Did he go home congratulating himself on a win? Was that it? Or did he wake up the next day with a hangover, mortified about how he'd behaved? But I tell you what I learned – because there are people like that, you can't afford to be nice. You know what I mean? You've got to step back a bit and be cold. These pricks are ruining it for everyone else.

On balance, the Fête des Jeunes Agriculteurs was a wonderful fair and I sold an awful lot of beer and bought a wildly expensive home-made cheese board, so, you know. That was the main point. But I was starting to think that maybe selling beer at these fêtes wasn't for me.

Interestingly, for such a booze fest, I've never seen the portable loos so clean, and this is because nobody used them. The surrounding fields were full of men and women peeing on the crops, but there wasn't so much as a queue at the actual loos. It's the country way.

I received an order in for beer from the *hypermarché* in Chinon. Two hundred bottles. If it sold well, they said, they'd order again and they'd order a higher quantity. This was brilliant news. I couldn't make enough beer to keep up with demand. I was winning! Although the summer wasn't without its challenges.

'Tommy, all your Biscuit Ale is out of date. So is your Clifton Porter.' A phone call from K'di Fermier, the local producers' shop in Chaveignes, sometime in June.

'But they can't be; I brewed those beers this month.' There was silence on the other end of the line. I continued, 'Aha, no, I see what's happened. The beer is fine. It's simply that the labels are out of date. There's really nothing to worry about.'

'The labels are out of date? But Tommy, we can't sell them with out-of-date labels. You'll have to change them.'

Have you ever done something so stupid that you can't really work out how you did it? You look back at it and it's a standalone wonder. It's almost beautiful – an inexplicable balls-up, up there on a plinth to be gazed at. A year or so before I'd had thousands of beer labels printed with one set use-by date on them – April 2019. Nowadays I have a blank space for a use-by date and I stamp it on at the time, depending on when the beer was brewed, but back then I didn't really know how it worked so I got a use-by date actually printed on the label. At the time I thought I'd use them all well before the date ran out, but for some reason I'd miscalculated and ordered far too many of them. As the year went on, I noticed that I was getting closer and closer to the use-by date but I didn't do anything about it. I kept putting them on my bottles. I'm telling you, I can't explain it. And suddenly the date on the bottles came and went and I still put the labels on. Hundreds of bottles with out-of-date labels on. I sort of knew, but at the same time I didn't. My eyes saw it and somewhere in the depths of my brain I knew I was supposed to do something about it, but it didn't register in the forefront of my mind. And the next thing I knew, shops and bars were calling me, furious that I'd sold them out-of-date beer.

Well, Margot still wasn't sleeping. Albert wasn't sleeping. I was so tired that I couldn't think straight and that was ultimately what it was. But you can't say that to people. Instead I had to go around to all the shops and bars and take back all the stock and relabel it while they looked at me like I was a moron. It was an enormous waste of time, but at the same time I still look back at what I did – something so very stupid – and, you know, I just marvel.

France is secular. They don't allow religion in their state institutions, so you don't have the equivalent of Church of England schools here. The state schools are non-religious.

And yet the French are more religious than the English. A lot of the villages around where we live feel very spiritual in a religious sense. These old churches still feel like the heart of the village, even though some are barely used now. Faye-la-Vineuse certainly has a godly stillness. Nueil-sous-Faye has an air of monastic peace and quiet. Even Braslou has a feeling of profundity, but you're never closer to God than when you pass through Marigny-Marmande. They've built this speed bump, you see, and I'm not kidding you, the sheer height of it – you scrape along the underside of heaven. It is like climbing the north face of the Eiger. At the top of it people fight for oxygen. There are lost tribes up there. You can pass an afternoon by the speed bump watching unsuspecting cars hitting it and launching off into fields left and right. When you drop off the other end, your ears pop.

As far as I can see, this all started in Chaveignes, just outside Richelieu, a couple of years previously. They were putting in place some new traffic-calming measures there just as you come into the village. I'm not sure if it's the same in the UK, but in France, since we've been here, there's been a relentless drive to install more and more elaborate traffic-calming measures at the entrances to villages. Now when you enter a village you have to be prepared for chicanes, traffic islands, loop the loops, crocodile-filled water pits. There's a rumour that there's a village in the Vendée that has installed a sphinx who asks you a riddle before you can continue on your journey.

In Chaveignes they went for a more traditional method – the speed bump. But what a speed bump. They built this speed bump just before the local garage there and it was so steep that when you drove over it for the first time, you thought you were having a seizure. They don't build

76

rounded speed bumps. They build ramps that shoot up at an extreme angle to a flat portion that runs along for eight feet or so, and then you drop off the other end on another ramp. You know, I don't think I'd ever thought I'd be describing speed bumps in such detail, yet here we find ourselves.

Now, I have no evidence for this, but it would be clever, wouldn't it, hypothetically, if the owner of the garage at Chaveignes, when he'd seen the workmen installing the speed bump, had sidled up to them and slipped them a few euros to make it a bit spicier than normal, because he real-ised that if a thousand cars a day drive over a speed bump of that ferocity, then at least a couple of them are going to have wheels fall off, and what should be right there, the other side of the speed bump, but a garage with wheels to spare? It's hypothetical, of course, but if I were that garage owner, I would be extremely pleased if I came up with that plan.

But from there something changed. The builder of these speed bumps got a taste for the extreme. You hear about this in sharks; something sparks it – perhaps they kill a human by accident, thinking they're a porpoise – but then they get the blood lust and they go on to kill again and again.

The next victim was Braslou. The speed bump they built there was an undertaking. I mean, it was essentially a wall. Since they built it, cars without four-wheel drive have been trapped there. There are people in Braslou who haven't left for years. They get friends and family to throw loaves of bread over the speed bump just so they can eat. After that, things went quiet for a little while, but just when car springs were starting to return to normal life, they struck again, and this time it was the big one. In Marigny-Marmande they must have put together a team of the finest international architects and they went one better than Braslou. They invented a new angle. The Marigny angle, just a bit steeper than vertical. The speed bump in Marigny-Marmande can be seen from the moon. Aircraft pilots use it to plot their paths.

Marigny-Marmande is the home of Scott and Elena, an English couple about our age with a little boy called Louis who's the same age as Albert. If you want to know how to successfully move to France and start a business, either do exactly as they did or do exactly the opposite of what we did. It's effectively the same thing. They did budgets and everything. They knew how much money they would have to make; they did meal plans – the lot. They're an inspiration. They have this incredible property, La Barauderie, just out from Marigny-Marmande – an old farmstead that had been converted into two luxury gîtes with a swimming pool. Scott's built a fire pit for roasting meat on. There's a trampoline and a play area for the kids. There's a little lake and a grand stone terrace with views across the overlapping hills of Marigny. It feels like you could be in Tuscany.

They moved out a couple of years after us. I first met them when I was selling beer at the Christmas truffle market in Marigny-Marmande. They'd heard there was another English couple and they wanted to come and meet us. They have no doubt regretted it ever since.

Like us, they'd had enough of working nine-to-five jobs in the UK and they moved out here. Unlike us, they formulated a proper plan to start a new life and they executed it. They've only been going a couple of years and their gîtes are almost always fully booked, and it's no surprise. They've put so much work into them. On several occasions we've thought about booking their gîtes for a holiday, even though they're ten minutes down the road.

You don't want to hang around exclusively with English

people if you move to France because the danger is you are only hanging around with them because you speak English and not because you have anything in common with them, but it's comforting to have some English friends you do have something in common with, especially if they're the same age as you and you like them and they do really, really good barbecues. Not long after, we met another English couple, Rupert and Annabel, who have a lovely gîte up in Luzé with their two girls, Florence and Emily, and, with Scott and Elena, we formed a little group. It was a sort of counselling group for life in France.

You move out here with the intention of making lots of French friends, and we had made friends. Damien and Celia, Monsieur and Madame Richard. Fred, Gramoui, Denis and Isabelle. God, it sounds desperate if I'm listing them, doesn't it? The guys at the market, of course – Sausage Woman and the like. Look, the truth is that it's hard to make meaningful friendships with French people if you are not fluent in French. Now, my French has improved since I started doing the market at Richelieu, not to the degree where I am fluent, but I'll tell you what has really improved: my *pretending to understand French*. Pretending to understand French is an art form. One that I have mastered. It's now perfectly possible for me to have five- or ten-minute chats with people at the market without having a clue what they're talking about and they never even realise it. You can do it too, with my new *Pretending to Understand French* three-part course. Firstly, learn a few stock phrases: if someone's been bleating on at you for a few minutes and you have no idea what they're talking about and then there's a pause, simply shrug and say something like, '*C'est comme ça*' – effectively, 'Well, that's how it is.' It doesn't really mean anything, and yet it could mean anything. It's beautiful. Or you could say – '*T'a raison*' – 'You're right.' People always like to hear that they are right. A more advanced technique when it's your turn to reply is to take a really deep breath and say '*ouai*', which means 'yep', but in one fluid motion you move the intonation around so it goes through a definitive 'yep' to a resigned 'yep' to a slightly questioning 'yep' and finishing on a philosophical, does anything really exist sort of 'yep', thus covering nearly all possible meanings. '*Ouuuuuuuuaaaaaiiii.*'

Secondly, you need to learn some non-committal noises. A semi-exasperated blowing of the cheeks. A shrug of the shoulders and a '*boff*' gets you a long way. I make a really good noise now. A sort of *unnngh*. Nobody knows what that means, but if you do it with confidence, they'll lap it up.

Punter in unintelligible French: 'What do you think of Macron's latest reforms?'

Me with zero understanding of what they've said: '*Ouuaaaiii.*'

'I see. I suppose it is worrying. But surely we have to do something?'

'*Unnnngh.*'

'You know what, you're right. I'll buy ten beers.'

'*Unnnnnnnnnnnnngh.*'

'OK, fine. There's really no need to bring my wife's limp into this. I'll take my business somewhere else.'

Thirdly, towards the end of the conversation, when you've used up all your stock phrases and noises, try and bring a passer-by into the conversation and, while they're talking, quietly tiptoe backwards until you can find a public bin to hide behind.

This is all fine for markets, but forming genuine friendships is hard. Our French isn't bad now, but talking to friends, making jokes, having sophisticated conversations is a whole different level. Now, some of you will be pointing out that I'd struggle to have a sophisticated conversation in any language, and to you I say *unnnnnnnnngh*. And also fart off.

With Damien and Celia and the other guys I so painfully listed we have developed genuine friendships because they have the patience and the forgiveness to get down to the conversations that matter, but it takes so much time to do that. If you spend enough time with people, then you can overcome language barriers and you get to something more fundamental, but it's hard to develop those relationships in general simply because people don't have the time. If you are invited to a dinner party and you're next to a French person you've not met before, you can't spend the entire evening saying '*unnnnngh*' (I know this because I have tried), and they are not there to babysit you for four hours so that they can get to the bottom of a God-awful joke you tried to make in your broken GCSE French.

It's about the subtleties of the language and you find yourself picking them up gradually without even knowing it; I mean, I'm already *ooh-la-la*-ing, and that is one of the base metrics of how well your French is coming on, but it takes time. But it was great to find some English friends like, Scott, Elena, Rupert and Annabel again.

Five terrified people sat on the stage as the crowd in the little town square watched, hushed with acute fascination.

'Shit. Have we stumbled across a public execution? Do they still do that here?' I whispered to Rose.

Rose didn't answer. She was bewitched. We all were. Scott and Elena, Rupert and Annabel, the children. We waited for the guillotine to be rolled out. But instead, each person was presented with an enormous, coiled, fat *boudin noir* – the French equivalent of a black pudding. Each one must have been a metre long. Then each person on the stage was given a bottle of wine and a wine glass.

'Three, two, one – EAT!' shouted a man in a cowboy hat, and all hell broke loose.

Men and women of all ages and backgrounds stuffed their faces with *boudin* and downed wine, sometimes directly from the bottle.

'Ah, right. This is exactly why I moved to France,' I whispered to Rose.

On stage the host shouted, 'Winner wins a washing machine!' and the crowd roared.

I'd seen signs for the Boudin Noir Festival in Rilly-sur-Vienne a few times since we'd been living in France, but I had never managed to persuade Rose to go because she didn't like the idea of eating a load of dried blood shoved into a pig's gut. But now, with Scott and Rupert as my allies, we used all our power to collectively whine until our partners agreed to come.

Back on stage some of the contestants were beginning to flag. The *boudin noirs* were seemingly endless. A young guy threw up and was escorted off stage, presumably to be shot and made into more *boudin noir*. Others gradually turned green and were rolled away. Finally, a quiet, bald man raised his hand somewhat meekly. An adjudicator came to check on him and declared him the winner. He handed him the washing machine, which turned out to be a bar of soap, and we all went to the *buvette* to have a bloody good drink while the children ran around in circles. When you move to the country you can start to miss a bit of culture, but then you go to the Foire aux Boudins at Rilly-sur-Vienne.

CHAPTER 4

'OK guys, thanks for coming. Albert, you can take notes, seeing as you've got a permanent marker. Actually, give me that, please Albert. ALBERT, FOR CHRIST'S SAKE.' Albert handed me the marker.

'Errr, Daddy, you're a pinky fart, Daddy,' he said earnestly.

'Right. Good. OK, welcome to our second ever Braslou Bière marketing meeting. I know it's a busy time for all of us, so I appreciate you making the effort,' I said. Rose groaned. Margot poured milk from her cereal onto the floor and watched with fascination as the dogs licked it up.

'So, quick recap – beer sales are going well. It's July, peak season, and we're selling more than ever before. The markets are full with tourists. We need to capitalise on that. Long story short, I'm going to get some t-shirts printed with our strapline on.'

'We have a strapline?'

'Yes, Rose, we agreed a strapline.'

'What did we agree?'

'You know what we agreed.'

'I know you came up with some terrible straplines. The worst of which you got printed on the back of your van before you'd even run them by me. I thought we'd decided they were all bad.'

'Um, Rose, there's no such thing as bad. There's only relativity, and the one we decided on was the best strapline, relatively speaking, compared to the other straplines. Except the one that had swearing in it, but you know – legal wrangles and all that, so I'm not using it any more for now.'

'What did we settle on?'

'*Braslou Bière – Yeah, It Cocking Did.*'

'Cocking, cocking, cocking!' said Albert gleefully.

'Hasn't Albert's speech come on?' I said.

'Coggy, coggy, coggy,' said Margot.

'You're getting there too, Margie,' I said.

'Erm, Daddy? You're an onion shark,' said Albert earnestly.

Rose frowned. 'Tommy, you should run these things by me before you make a decision.'

'OK, Rose. Right. We've got the Nocturne Gourmande coming up in Richelieu in August. It's potentially our biggest fête of the year. Damien has agreed to help again. Current feedback from Damien is that we're a nightmare to work with.'

'We?' Said Rose.

'This is our chance to prove to him that we can be organised. We have two weeks to plan. Albert, I want you to draw up a list of action points and responsibilities. Margot – just keep doing what you're doing, everyone is happy with your development. Maybe less screaming all night, but otherwise good. Rose–'

'I could make a list of everything you need to do before the fête," said Rose.

"What do I always say, Rose? If God had wanted us to make lists, he would have given us Biro fingers.'

'You've never said that.'

Rose was right. I had never said that. But I didn't want Rose writing lists of things I needed to do and I had no intention of running things by her. It was my brewery. It was the only thing that I really had control of. The thing about me is I'm easily persuaded. I'm the sort of guy that automatically thinks someone else's suggestion is better than my own, so in everyday life there's very little that I really have a piece in. And the thing is, I do have some good ideas. I have some terrible ones too, but I have some good ones as well, but it always feels like my ideas get overridden. I knew this about myself, so I wanted to keep everyone else out of the brewery and then I would be able to do it my way. I didn't need a feeble list to organise myself.

In among all the fêtes, the kids were at home for the summer holidays. In France the children start school at 3-years-old and Margot was in nursery during the school term.

'Um, Rose, as a parent, you can either sit back and coast, just be happy to let the school take care of your child's education and you know, maybe they'll turn out OK, who knows? Or you can take responsibility for their mental and moral growth. It takes commitment and effort, but you can provide a rich, stimulating and above all intellectual environment for them to learn in. I know what side I'm on. The question is, what side are you?'

'Yes, but Tommy, he's too young to go and see the monster trucks.'

'Rose, this is a once-in-a-lifetime experience. And Albert will get a kick out of it as well.'

There are various roadshows that pass through Richelieu. Circuses and all that. One day at the roundabout in

Chaveignes a trailer full of monster trucks was parked up. There was to be a monster-truck derby on the grounds near the campsite in Richelieu. A poster boasted of exotic, fat-tyred machines leaping hundreds of feet through the air. There were rings of fire and monster trucks of all varieties. We were so excited, Rose agreed to let us go.

Albert and I arrived on a hot August evening to a half-full stand of expectant Richelais. Slightly odd – the monster trucks that we'd seen on the trailer at the roundabout were still on the trailer outside the ground. Surely they should be unloaded and ready to do some serious monster trucking, right?

We queued up to buy tickets from a caravan. A middle-aged man strutted around in a racing suit, which did a good job of concealing his podge, and a wireless headset and microphone as if he was Madonna mid-concert. Never had anyone been so proud to be wearing a race suit and headset. I very much got the impression that if he had his way, the show would have just been him strutting around in his race suit and headset. As it turned out, large parts of the show were exactly that.

We took our seats on a hastily erected wooden grandstand. The audience were hushed with anticipation. Would monster trucks burst onto the scene from every direction – jumping – roaring – crushing rows of cars, flames shooting out of their exhausts? The guy in the race suit and headset walked slowly, confidently out to the middle. He was a hero. A god. What the hell was about to happen? Monster trucks dropping from the sky? Well, not quite. I believe what happened next was the headset guy gave us a lecture on seat belts.

With the crowd suitably revved to a frenzy, finally some motor action! A man in a Renault hatchback that had recently been driven out of the local breaker's yard circled the showground, hanging out of the window with his fist raised like a king returning from a triumphant crusade. He then did what was effectively a high-speed reverse park. There was confusion and disappointment in the crowd. Then he toured the showground again with his fist raised to absolutely zero applause. Never have I been so proud of the Richelais.

'Where are the monster trucks, Daddy?' said Albert.

'They'll come,' I said. I was now pretty certain they weren't going to come.

Next up, after another talk from headset guy on road safety, literally the one thing we weren't here to see, were some youths on quad bikes doing wheelies. Like the first guy, they started and ended by riding past the half-full grandstand with their fists raised to absolute silence. I mean, I couldn't do what they did on those quad bikes, so there was that, but then I couldn't operate a canned tuna-fish plant. No one gives the canned tuna-fish plant operator a round of applause every time he cans some tuna fish, do they? Or do they?

'Where are the monster trucks, Daddy?'

Next up, a guy in a car driving through some planks of wood that they'd set on fire. I mean, Christ alive – the build-up headset man gave that one. And then the guy drives an old banger through some planks of wood, and they all run out afterwards to put the few scattered flames out like the place was going to explode and wipe out civilisation.

'Where are the monster trucks, Daddy?' demanded Albert.

They were doing their best to try to sell it. The man in charge of the petrol can was particularly committed, and I admired him for that, seeing as that seemed to be his only role. He poured petrol on the ground from an old jerry can and would light the match and throw it as if he were a musketeer duelling his arch nemesis. But no amount of flourish could hide the fact he was just lighting a bit of petrol on old waste ground.

Then a guy driving an old banger rolled two wheels up a ramp at a speed so slow that you needed a time-lapse camera to see it moving, until finally the car tottered over onto its roof. He did it so slowly that it actually couldn't have been any less impressive, and they all rushed out to the car as if he might be dead. Spoiler – he wasn't dead. I'm telling you, I've seen far more dangerous driving on a daily basis at the supermarket car park in Chaveignes. And so it continued, until at last – the finale.

From one end of the field a spluttering of an engine, and lo and behold, much to our collective surprise, a genuine monster truck appeared. Not one of the ones on the trailer parked outside, of course. It was almost as if the monster trucks on the trailer were actually just some broken-down cars that they'd painted in lurid colours and attached old tractor wheels to. No, but this one looked impressive none the less – enormous wheels and painted up a like a US police car. Except it wasn't a monster truck – or rather, as the man with the headset explained, it was a monster truck, but the trucks that you see on television – the ones that roar and jump twenty feet in the air – the monster trucks that race around the tracks and do backflips and other extraordinary things – they weren't actually monster trucks. They were monster racing trucks – this was a proper monster truck. And proper monster trucks, he explained with pride, could do none of those things. He then proceeded to roll his monster truck agonisingly slowly onto an old car.

'Who wants to see it again?' he shouted excitedly from atop his perch. No one responded. In his head, he heard a rapturous, 'We do!' He reversed the monster truck off the car and very, very slowly drove up onto the now squashed car once again. A triumphant raised hand out of the monster-truck window to absolute silence and that was that. I bought Albert a flag and we returned home somewhat confused.

Brew day: Biscuit Ale

Malts
- Pale malt
- Vienna
- Cara Munich
- Crystal (medium)

Hops
- Magnum
- Barbe Rouge

Yeast
- AEB American West Coast

Biscuit Ale is named after my Aunt Maggi's dog, Biscuit, now sadly deceased. It's a malty, amber ale (here they call it an *ambrée*) that's gone through more iterations than I can remember. It started off being made with Nugget and Hull Melon hops, a good dose of Munich malt and an Abbaye yeast, but by now I was using an American-ale yeast, Magnum and Barbe Rouge hops and Vienna and Cara Munich malts. This is meaningless to half of you, isn't it?

Skip to the next paragraph if so. I was really starting to get somewhere with it now. It was never going to be my most popular beer, because the popular beers are blonde beers and IPAs, but I was very fond of it. It was a clever beer. It's much harder to try and balance a malty beer in my opinion, because there were no huge hop flavours to hide behind. *Ambrées* often have a tame, sweet character because of the maltiness, but I had a Licorn *ambrée* at Bruno's bar once that had a real bitterness to it that made it more interesting. I began aiming for something like that.

I mashed in quite high, 69° C, which I was OK with, because I think a higher mash temperature extracts more of the malty flavours. As I stirred the mash, I was still thinking about the previous day's monster-truck show. Looking back on it, there was a clue I should have picked up on. Along the bottom of the poster they wrote that it was 'under new management'. I realise now this was the only way they might persuade people who'd seen it the last time they toured to come back again. This is a monster-truck show that will be forever under new management. Anyway – highly recommended. If they come to your town, definitely go and see them. They've essentially taken a scene from a Saturday night on a Manchester housing estate and toured it around France.

The brew was going surprisingly well. I'd yet to flood anything or indeed receive any major electric shocks. After the mash, I moved the wort to the copper and added my hops along with two kilos of brown sugar. I was aiming for a stronger beer – 6 per cent vol – so I needed to add the extra sugar. Extra sugar can thin the beer out, but this beer had plenty of Cara Munich and Crystal to give it the mouthfeel.

An hour later I started passing the wort into the fermenter.

You need the wort to be sufficiently cooled by the time you add the yeast, so that the yeast can live in it. Depending on the yeast, this is between 12° C and anything up to the high twenties. To adjust the temperature that the beer comes into the fermenter, you have to adjust the flow of the water coming into the plate chiller. It's tricky because every time you adjust it, it takes a few minutes for those adjustments to affect the temperature of the wort heading into the fermenter. You have to be extremely precise with your changes as well; opening the tap a millimetre or two can make a huge difference. I had just begun this process when Albert, sitting on his pushbike, poked his head round the door.

'Daddy, Margot is picking cherries,' Albert said.

'OK, Albert. Make sure she doesn't eat the stones.'

'Daddy, you're a hot cross poo.'

Albert whizzed out of the brewery. I thought about it for a moment. Actually, maybe it wasn't a good idea for her to be eating cherries. She was eight months old. I left the brewery momentarily.

'Margie, don't eat the— JESUS CHRIST! MARGOT, GET DOWN FROM THERE! ACTUALLY, DON'T GET DOWN FROM THERE. I'LL GET YOU DOWN.'

Thirty metres away, the other side of the garden, Margot had crawled to the top of a ten-foot stepladder and was reaching precariously for cherries in the trees. I sprinted across the garden to save her.

'Margie, it's OK. I'm here now. Just stay still.' Margot giggled and threw cherries at me as I climbed the ladder as delicately as I could.

When I returned to the brewery, the fermenter was half full. I checked the temperature of the wort in the fermenter and it was way too hot. I adjusted the tap on the plate chiller to try and lower the temperature as best I could, but by the time it was done it was still too warm to pitch the yeast, so I left the doors of the brewery open overnight to try and cool it some more and pitched the yeast the next day.

And that is how you brew Biscuit Ale.

August. Hot – 39° C. The Nocturne Gourmande in Richelieu. A festival of food and drink held at night. Shitshow doesn't do it justice. Shitberg, maybe. However you want to describe it using the word shit, it was a disaster. It was a shitnami. It was *Shits in the Mist* starring Meryl Shit.

'It's almost started already, and you haven't even packed up the van, Tommy. We're going to be late.' Damien was disappointed, but not surprised. He'd turned up from work at 5.45 p.m. expecting us – quite reasonably, seeing as I had been home all afternoon – to be ready to go. He was wrong. Damien often helps me with fêtes and the like when he's not working. He never asks for any money.

The Nocturne Gourmande is a huge event round here. It's an annual night market in Richelieu where all the restaurants set up stands around the main square and they reach back into the early 1980s to find a DJ for the evening. By 7 p.m. the square is packed with thousands of thirsty, line dancing clients. They love a bit of line dancing. It's the busiest Richelieu gets. If the weather is good, it's an absolute open goal when it comes to selling beer. It's hard to get a stand there, but for some reason Fred the policeman, the man who is in charge of these things in Richelieu, seemed to want me there. He held a spot open for me even though I was weeks late with my application. This should have been the perfect end to the season.

'I'm tired, Damien. I don't want to go.' Poor me. I

was tired. Margot still wasn't sleeping. I was hoping that Damien wouldn't turn up. I hadn't got anything ready. The last few weeks had been relentless. Beer was flying out. I was everywhere – delivering, selling, brewing. I'd been at Richelieu market that morning and now I was tired. Poor little Tommy. If only Rose had made me a list. I cursed my non Biro fingers.

'Come on.' When Damien tells you to come on, you come on. That was that. We began loading the Tub of Thunder (TVNM) with everything we had. Any kegs I could find. Then we stuck in the pallet bar that Damien had made and the two beer pumps. Gramoui, a friend of mine from up the top of the hill above Braslou, had a beer pump that he lent me in exchange for a couple of bottles of beer.

Damien jumped into the passenger seat and the Tub of Thunder burst into life. Whenever you start the Tub of Thunder it leaves a black exhaust mark on the ground – a sort of 'I was here' statement. In thousands of years archaeologists will find black marks all over the driveway and they will be able to plot all the places I parked the van on the driveway and make a programme about it for Channel 5.

Burt was furious that Damien had taken his seat in the Tub of Thunder. To this day he hasn't forgiven him. That's Burt for you, though. He holds a grudge.

We set off down the road to Richelieu, leaving Burt in the garden already working on an intricate ten-year plot to get his revenge on Damien. Five hundred metres on and there were two red lights on the dashboard. I put my hand on the engine cover, which in a J9 is handily situated in the middle of the cab. It was nuclear. We pulled over and hissed to a stop.

One of the lights was definitely the oil warning light.

This often came on. This was like an old friend. The other, I think, was the engine light. That came on quite regularly too, but I felt like we had less of a connection. Normally they alternated. They never came on at the same time. No, this was not good. I looked at Damien. He shrugged. I started the engine again and carried on.

Another kilometre or so and there was a large clunk. Something had fallen off the van. Through the black smoke I caught a glimpse of it in the rear-view mirror, lying in the road as we trundled on. Now, normally when something falls off the van, I see it as a good thing. The thing with the van is it often starts making grinding noises accompanied by the smell of burning rubber or metal, but they usually go away after a while and it seems to me the van is just working through its problems. Likewise, when things fall off the van – bits of metal, nuts, bolts, doors – it has become lighter and therefore more efficient. I see it as a sort of natural evolution – it's just getting rid of unnecessary baggage – not holding on to the past. We could all learn from the Tub of Thunder in this respect. But this time it wasn't good. The van was now making a rotational clacking sound.

We continued at a cautionary speed. The van made it to Richelieu and hobbled into the Place du Marché with steam pouring from the engine. Because we were so late, all the other stalls were set up, so I couldn't get my van into the square. We had to park over the road behind the square. I checked the van to see if I could work out what had fallen off. It was immediately apparent – half the tyre tread had disappeared from the front left wheel. The lights on the dashboard, it seemed, were an altogether different problem. It must have been coincidence it had all happened at once. I had no time to worry about that now. We had

94

to shift everything from the back of the van twenty metres to where our stand was. Twenty metres doesn't sound like much, but when you've got so much heavy equipment and you're already shattered and it's still 38° C, it's hard. Kegs, beer pumps, boxes of bottles, a bar. And all this while the market was already underway.

Damien had made the bar out of pallets for his wedding. French weddings are better than British ones. No offence everyone who has married in Britain. French weddings last a weekend, minimum, and there's none of the approval-seeking of British weddings. I'm not saying British weddings are bad – some are good fun – but when you go to a British wedding, you always get the feeling you are a pawn in somebody's plan to show somebody else quite specific that this wedding is better than theirs. In France there's much less of that. And you don't think of the French as a particularly wild nation, but when they celebrate, they really commit. Nothing stops at 11 p.m. like it might do in the UK. In fact, nothing really gets started until 11 p.m., and then it goes and goes, and everyone – young and old – goes with it until it's done. That might be four in the morning. That might be eight in the morning. It goes until it's done. And then it goes again the next day.

After his wedding, Damien had given the bar to me to use for fêtes and the like. We take it apart to fit it in the van and then assemble it when we get to an event. The problem is, instead of storing it in the barn, I'd left it in the garden to warp in the sun and rain and it was increasingly difficult to put together. It had been designed specifically to fit my beer pump and Gramoui's, but because it was warped and twisted, it was harder and harder to fit the beer pumps in. I'd forgotten the spanner we needed to attach the beer taps, and I had to run around asking other stallholders if they had one. It took us half an hour of fiddling around before we'd got the pumps installed in the bar. Then worse.

'You haven't chilled Gramoui's beer pump.'

'No. Why? We just need to plug it in and it will be fine.'

'Tommy, it takes three hours for Gramoui's beer pump to get cold enough to serve the beer.' I hadn't realised this. This should definitely have been on the list. I had a new beer pump that chilled the beer almost instantly using technology I'd love to explain to you at this exact minute, but I've never bothered to investigate, whereas Gramoui's was an old-style beer pump that worked by passing the beer lines through a chilled water reservoir to cool the beer. You have to pump the beer from kegs at a very low temperature to avoid the beer foaming, you see. It turns out that it takes several hours to chill the water reservoir in Gramoui's pump sufficiently to cool the beer.

Just when it looked like we were down to one pump, Damien had a brainwave. He disappeared and came back with a large bucket of ice from the hotel in the square and dumped it directly in the reservoir, and not long after it was pouring beer. It was lucky he fixed it, because my pump wasn't working properly. It was foaming too much. I found out later that one of the seals was missing from a connection, so air was getting in, but at the time it meant I had to pour beer really slowly and leave half of it on the floor. Then the crowds arrived. Queues of people snaking back into the centre of the square. I didn't really see much of the fête, because I had my back turned to it, pouring beer for four hours flat. We sold so much beer that night. It was awful; I was covered in stale old beer, my feet were stuck to the ground. My shoes were full of IPA. It was stressful, hot. As the night went on, people became drunk and surly. People were upset about the time it took to pour beer from the frothing pump. We ploughed on regardless. With Damien there I knew we'd be all right. Finally it was midnight. The fête had officially closed an hour before, but there were still people buying beer until we switched the pumps off. We'd made good money. I didn't enjoy it for one second, but we'd done well.

But it confirmed to me that I disliked selling beer at fêtes like this. I'm not cut out to be a frontman. As the van limped home through the darkness, I thought to myself, *It's time to change the tactics.* Selling to shops was so much easier. I'd made more from that one order from the hypermarket in Chinon than I'd made in an entire day at some of the quieter fêtes. You turn up, drop the beer off and the money arrives in your account a few days later. No drunken twats trying to get free beer out of you. No dragging equipment around in the heat. If I could just get some more big-money orders like that, my life would be better.

Three chickens arrived. I assumed it was part of Rose's pregnancy cravings, which was odd, because she hadn't been pregnant for six months. Albert named them Chickaloo, Petite and Nellus.

We'd had two chickens before – little Chinese bantams. Burt had eaten them. This time we got big fat Sussex chickens. Burt had his eye on them from the start. I don't like chickens on the whole. They lack empathy. I may be expecting too much.

Richelieu market had been excellent once more. August is a strange month in France, because most French go on holiday, often for the entire month. *But who's manning the shops and service stations and hospitals if everyone is on holiday? I hear you ask.* Well, you'd assume they'd have a clever system, but in a lot of cases things are just shut. I wasn't on holiday and the market was full of tourists, while patients lay on the operating table in empty hospitals wondering when their surgeon would return.

Luckily the bakery, Subileau, was open too.

'Two croissants, a *pain tradition* and a croissant, please,' I said, stopping by on my way home.

'Anything else?' said Nadège.

'Um. Yes. What's that one there?' I said.

'That's an artisanal bread with walnuts in it.'

'I see. Walnuts. Interesting. I'll have one more croissant. Also, I was wondering if Sébastien could show me how he makes his *pain tradition* sometime?'

'Yeah, sure. No problem. Come by on Wednesday if you like,' said Nadège. This took me by surprise. I was expecting her to fob me off with an excuse. There was no way she'd let me into the back of the bakery, I thought. You see, at that particular bakery, the Boulangerie Subileau, along the road from the chocolate-orange roundabout (it looks like a Terry's Chocolate Orange – the French don't understand this reference) to Richelieu in Chaveignes, an innocuous looking place really, there was magic going on.

'OK. Wednesday it is then.' I screwed my eyes up at her.

'Great. If that's all, we'll see you then.' She played me with a straight bat.

'Right. Actually, what's that loaf there?'

'That's a multi-grain bread.'

'Interesting. Very interesting. Another croissant please.' Pretty much since we arrived I'd developed a croissant habit that rapidly took over my life. You know those before and after pictures of crack addicts they use to show you the danger of drugs? Beforehand the guy looks chubby and happy and after all the crack he looks gaunt and miserable. Well, my croissant addiction was like that, but the other way around.

I couldn't wait till Wednesday. I've talked before about the loaf of bread called *pain tradition* they make there (read the first book, you cheap bastards). It's unsurpassable. You can take your sourdoughs and shit off, because you won't find a better loaf, especially when it's not long from the oven and still warm and you spread salty Brittany butter on it.

Their croissants are fantastic too. Croissants were originally developed by the Austrians to celebrate the time they stuck it to the Ottoman Empire (hence the crescent shape to mock the crescent on the Ottoman flag), but the French got their hands on them in the eighteenth century and improved them as they most commonly improve food – by adding slabs of butter. I can't think of two words that complement each other more perfectly than 'slab' and 'butter'. I have a few thoughts on butter. We know that butter is what milk could have been if it had made better life choices. We know that. That's a given. But butter is more than that. It's more valuable than gold. It's the heaviest substance in the universe. It doesn't show up in photographs. I've no idea what I'm talking about.

You'll find different versions of croissants right across France, but the best ones are crunchy on the outside, chewy in the middle and taste of slabs of butter. The Subileau croissants are among the best.

Everything they do at the Subileau bakery is superb. But the *pain tradition*, no, it's too good. It's so perfectly balanced.

The crust, the chew. And it's not even trying, that's the thing. Sourdough loaves are always trying to show each other how artisanal they are. The Subileau *pain tradition* is just *there*. I'm telling you now, something is going on in that bakery, and I am onto them. Mystical elves. An oven that is a portal to another realm. A mixer with blades of unicorn horn (great name for a band).

Since I cottoned on that magic was taking place there, I would arrive for my twice-daily croissant stop, pick up some *pain tradition* and make small talk with Nadège, the woman who runs the bakery along with her partner Sébastien, while trying to peek behind her into the kitchen area to see if I could see any magic puffs of glitter – the telltale signs of an elf kingdom – but there was nothing. Now they had invited me in, and I was about to expose them once and for all for what they really were – sorcerers from the craters of the moon or something along those lines. The exact details would be revealed during the visit, I thought.

When Nadège ushered me in, I was disappointed. It was immediately obvious there had been a major cover-up operation. Sébastien was waiting to show me how the bakery worked. A large bread oven on the right-hand side, four times the size of a normal oven. Some outsized dough mixers on the left. Swept piles of white flour on the floor. I walked round the place, tapping surfaces, lifting pots up to see if a baking pixie was hiding underneath. Checking the blades of the mixer for a pearlescent unicorn hue. Nothing. It was as if he was a very good baker who loved his craft and had the knowledge and experience to be excellent at what he did. It was as if he was that. And yet I saw a *pain tradition* on the counter and immediately I remembered it was not possible to make something so perfect, no matter how good he was. No, they had either found some kind of space dust in a meteor that had crashed through their roof or a garden gnome had been hit by lightning, come to life and had whispered them some secrets.

Sébastien showed me the difference between the *pain tradition* and a normal French bread – the big fluffy golden ones that we recognise as French bread in the UK.

'OK, *pain tradition* is made with different flour; it's flour we get from a family-run mill, with no preservatives in it. That's why you won't see it in the supermarkets – they need to add preservatives to their bread.'

'Right. And that dust you're adding there. Is that ground rhino horn or has it come from outer space? I suppose what I am trying to say is, do you add moon dust?'

'It's salt. You need to add a really good pinch of salt crystals.'

'*Touché*,' I said.

'To get the texture we don't knead the dough too much – unlike the big golden French sticks, the idea isn't to get as much air in as you can. The inside wants to be chewy.'

'So you're telling me this has something to do with quantum mechanics? Other alternative realities, yes?'

'No. Then, to make the long stick shape, you simply elongate the dough and then fold over the sides on the top. With a French stick you turn the dough over to hide the seam this creates underneath the bread when it bakes, and you slash it across the top to get the diagonal ridges and let it rise, but with a *pain tradition* you leave the seam on top and this creates the long ridge that runs along the top. It's baked at two-hundred and eighty degrees Celsius.'

'I see. And where exactly did you learn to make this bread?' I had him now.

'I got the recipe from the bakery I did my apprenticeship at. It's interesting – you'll find every bakery makes its *pain tradition* slightly differently.'

'It is interesting, very interesting – especially when I open this cupboard to reveal your secret ingredient, a dodo egg!' I opened the cupboard. There was no egg.

'Here's a *pain tradition* on the house. Let me know if you want to know anything else,' said Sébastien.

'You win this time, Subileau's, with your magnificent bakery, but this is only the start,' I said to myself as I chewed the end of the loaf in the car home.

'*Bonjour* Patrick, it's Tommy. I make the beer in Braslou. We met at the asparagus festival,' I said down the phone. It was time for the final part of my plan – the wine and beer distributor and possible secret agent that I met at the asparagus market in Braslou.

'Ah! Tommy. How are you? I've been meaning to call you.'

'Yes, look, I was wondering if you were still interested in buying my beer. I'd like to do fewer fêtes and things and sell more to professionals.'

'Absolutely. Look, I'll come over with my colleague next week and we can discuss it face to face.'

'Brilliant. There was something else. There's this over-weight dog you see, looks like a sort of rolled-up futon with angry eyes, and I need him – how do you say? – disappeared. You understand me, Patrick?'

'No, I'm not sure I do.'

'Do you own a poisonous dart-gun, Patrick?'

'No. OK, see you next week Tommy.'

*

The problem with the tyre on the van was obvious, but the lights on the dashboard, the red-hot engine and the steaming was a different thing. I managed to get the van to the Peugeot garage in Île-Bouchard. A young mechanic came out, took one look at this van that was more than twice his age, and beat a hasty retreat. Then the owner of the garage, Alain, came out. Alain was a wiry old mechanic, maybe in his sixties, who smoked almost as much as my van. He knew Peugeot J9s from the first time round. He was exactly who I needed.

'There's no water in your radiator,' said Alain after a cursory glance at the van.

'Aha. I very much suspected as much.' I nodded. I didn't know the van had a radiator. Presumably to take the edge off in the winter months.

Alan continued. 'It might have a leak. On a side note, the hydraulic fluid is low too. You might have a leak there as well.'

Hmm. Hydraulic fluid. Didn't sound important.

'Well, can you make it work again?' I said. Alan poured some water into the radiator.

'Yes,' he said. 'It is fixed.'

'Aha! Water. I should have known. All life is water. Wasn't it Anaxagoras who said that? Or the other guy. Anaximander? One of those Greek guys, right?'

Alain handed me the keys.

Anthony, another mechanic I knew who worked there, very kindly put on an old tyre he had lying around to tide me over till I got some proper ones for it. It was slightly smaller than the rest of my tyres. I noticed on the way back that with a slightly smaller tyre on the left front, the van had never driven better.

CHAPTER 5

'You can't park here, Tommy.'

'I'm just being Italian, Rose.'

'You're being inconsiderate. You're practically blocking the road. There's parking spaces just down there.'

'I'm being a genuine human living on my desires, Rose. They will respect me for that.'

A white van squeezed through the gap I left and the driver mouthed something at me involving lots of syllables and shook his head.

'See, Rose. He respects me.'

Ever since we'd come back from Italy, I'd been inspired to drive terribly. I parked where I wanted. I cut people up on the inside lane on the motorway. I went the wrong way down one-way streets and I comforted myself that, deep down, everyone respected me for it.

I was at the bank to see Monsieur Jean, my bank manager. We wanted investment.

One of the big criticisms of my beer was that it had too much deposit in the bottle. It's very off-putting if a load of sludge pours out into your glass. One way of clearing the beer is to 'cold crash' it. That means that you reduce the temperature of the beer in the fermenter down to around 1° C for a few days. This helps lots of the particles suspended in the beer to drop to the bottom of the fermenter, thus clearing the beer. That's the theory. It's quite easy to do if you're home-brewing because you ferment in little buckets and you can just chuck them in the fridge, but when you have bigger fermenters – 200- or 400-litre fermenters – that is a lot of liquid to chill, and you'd need an enormous fridge the size of a bus to fit them in. A better solution is to get a jacketed (double-walled) fermenter and a powerful chiller unit and then, when you want to reduce the temperature of the fermenter, you pump cold water mixed with glycol from the chiller through the jacket of the fermenter and that drops the temperature down. Being able to directly control the temperature like this also meant I could keep my fermentation temperatures under control. It was expensive to get this stuff – a new jacketed stainless-steel 400-litre fermenter and a big powerful chiller unit – thousands of pounds, but I knew my beer was a long way from good enough. It sold well locally, but it didn't stand up to the other artisan brewers in the area. It was still essentially home brew. If I wanted to sell it to the wider region, I needed to make more professional beer and this was the next step.

'Ha ha! *Bonjour* Monsieur Barnes, how can I help you?' said Monsieur Jean as he welcomed me into his office. Monsieur Jean was deranged. You could tell from the huge smile on his face. It was clear from the start we'd get on well.

'Yes, well, I have a microbrewery in Braslou, and we need to upgrade our equipment.'

'I love beer!' said Monsieur Jean.

'Me too!' I said. Together we thought about beer for a few seconds. 'Well, I would like a loan to get a chiller unit and a new fermenter.'

'Oh yes. Brilliant. How much do you want?'

'About five thousand euros?'

'OK, let me see your accounts.' He looked at my accounts. Then he punched some stuff into the computer. 'OK. It's done.'

'What?'

'It will arrive in seven days. Tell me more about beer.'

Salut, Tommy. Thank you for inviting us over.' The afternoon was oppressively hot in late August, so we sought refuge on a bench under the trees in the garden. Patrick, the distributor of beer I'd met at the fête in Braslou, was here to talk business. He was immaculately dressed in a dark turtleneck, as if he came straight from uncovering a Soviet spy ring in 1960s London. 'We love the story of your brewery. Bumbling English guy comes over to the middle of nowhere and starts making beer.'

'Yes,' said Laurent, Patrick's colleague. 'English fool in the French countryside haplessly blundering his way through life while making beer.'

I was a little taken aback, but Patrick continued.

'We'd love to sell your beer. We sell to a network of high-end restaurants and bars in Paris and the surrounding area. Can you give us a price per bottle? What you have to remember is we are middlemen, so we need to be able to make a profit on the beer as well. But we would buy your beer in pallets. We're talking large quantities.'

'Yeah sure – how about one euro sixty a bottle.' I plucked the number out of the air. It sounded quite high to me but I was playing hard ball.

'It's a deal,' said Patrick, delighted.

'Ah, crap,' I said. We shook hands on it.

I reflected on it and maybe I should have aimed a bit higher, but I was still very happy. I was making less of a profit on the bottles, but they would be buying in large quantities. That meant less time at fêtes and markets, less driving around. All I had to do was brew and bottle beer and they would turn up, buy most of it and go and do all the hard work selling it. After a summer of selling at fêtes, this was exactly what I wanted.

'What beers do you have available at the moment?' asked Patrick

'I've got no beer at all Patrick, I've sold it all, but all of my fermenters are full. I will have two thousand bottles of blonde beer and Biscuit ale available in a month's time.'

'Excellent,' said Patrick. 'Call me when they are ready and we will come and get them.'

'Superb. Now, look.' I got my phone out. 'This is a picture of the dog. He gets fed at nine a.m. every morning round the back of the barn. The area is not overlooked by CCTV.' I winked at him.

'It's a nice dog. OK, stay in touch, Tommy.'

As Patrick and Laurent got back in their car, I reflected that these would be the first beers that I had cold crashed properly and the first time I had used my new 400-litre double-walled fermenter. They would be the best, most professional beers I had made up to this point. This time last year beer sales had nosedived. Now, with the orders from the distributor and the big supermarket, if anything I would be selling more beer through winter than I had in summer. We were actually going to be OK. Oh, and finally, incredibly, Margot had started sleeping.

But wait, you say. *If everything is so perfect, how come we are only halfway through the book?* Oh, take a wild guess.

CHAPTER 6

Early September. The new blonde beer was almost done fermenting, which was a relief, because I was out of beer and I had orders to fill. The *hypermarché* in Chinon had called and they wanted another 200 bottles. Patrick, my brand-new distributor, was waiting on as much beer as I could supply. I had two local shops and several local bars waiting for the blonde.

Bottling day at Braslou Bière works like this. The night before, as I guzzle Fred's red wine, I tell Rose I will be up at 5 a.m. to start bottling. The next day I wake up at 5 a.m., curse at the moon and go back to sleep till 7 a.m. Then I get up and wrestle with the kids for an hour until they've eaten a couple of spoons of Weetabix and got their clothes on back to front. I boil three litres of water and add sugar. More sugar for Belgian beers – less for IPAs and stouts. The more sugar, the more carbonated the beer will eventually be. I ferry two obstreperous children off to their school and crèche in the medieval streets of Richelieu. I curse at the sun. I come home, drink a coffee with the potency to revive the Roman Empire, a coffee with the power to refloat the *Mary Rose*, and I stomp over the driveway to the brewery.

It's musty and dim. It's bad for the lungs, that brewery. I walk to and from the brewery several times. Up and down the stairs, pacing round and round. In the same way that dolphins circle a shoal of fish to corral them into a tight circle before they feed on them, so I have to walk round and round, corralling my disparate thoughts together to make something intelligible. Finally, I am semi-lucid. I begin rinsing the bottles in sanitiser. I step outside for a moment and I curse at the sky and everything in it. I run cleaner and sanitiser through the bottling equipment – bacteria in a bottle could ruin that bottle of beer, and if there's anything in the bottling equipment, then that could ruin all the beer, so you've got to make sure everything is cleaned and sanitised. Even the bottle tops. I curse at Michael Bublé, and somewhere, Michael Bublé curses back.

I transfer the beer from the fermenter into another stainless-steel vat and add the sugar solution that I boiled earlier. Once in the bottle, the sugar solution will be fermented by any yeast that remains suspended in the beer. Part of the fermentation process is the creation of CO_2, and this gas will carbonate the beer. It's called bottle conditioning. That's how we make fizzy beer traditionally, you see. Industrial breweries will likely artificially carbonate all their beer because it's quicker and easier to control, but if you bottle condition your beer, it continues to live and develop in the bottle and it remains stable for up to two years. Maybe more.

I curse at Burt. I curse at Burt. I curse at Burt. I pour a bit of beer to taste and I begin bottling. At that time, I had a plucky little bottle filler called the Enolmatic, which is home-brew equipment really, but it did the job. I have a manual bottle capper and a labelling machine you operate with a handle. It's about as unsophisticated as you can get. When visitors come to see the brewery, I say to them, 'It's very artisanal – in fact, it's *too* artisanal!' and I guffaw at my wit. They stare at me like I'm a prick until I've stopped laughing. 'But seriously, though, it's very artisanal,' I say and quickly we move on.

Although the brewery has a 400-litre capacity, you lose beer at every stage: some boils off in the copper; some gets left in the hop sludge; when you transfer from the fermenter to the bottling vat you leave a fair bit in the fermenter with the yeast; and when you bottle with the Enolmatic, it loses several litres of beer in the process due to foaming. So I normally make between 300 and 360 litres and I split it in half to bottle, so I might bottle 180 litres, and that can take me five hours or more from start to finish. It's the worst job in the brewing process, it's mundane, but when it's finished and you have 500 bottles neatly labelled and packed in boxes, it's satisfying.

And so this morning I did all the usual things. I even cursed at Burt an extra time and tried to hit him with a fly swatter and a child's shoe, and I settled down to bottle. But when I poured the first little bit to taste, the beer tasted sour to me. Now, beer never tastes that great at this stage; it's not carbonated, for starters, it might be warm and it is still young. It will develop a lot more in the bottle, so it's not necessarily a bad thing if it doesn't taste that great. But this taste was something different and I knew it, but I did that thing again that I always do, and that I hate about myself. I needed the beer to be good; after a really good summer selling beer, I was low on stock and everybody was waiting for the new batch. I badly needed some more blonde beer to sell, so I told myself it was OK. I told myself it might have been bitterness, not sourness that I tasted. It's quite hard to tell at a low level. There were alarms going off in my head and I ignored them. I always do that. I bury my head in the sand. I recited my mantra – *'It will probably be all right'* – and I bottled it regardless.

A few days later it was time to bottle my latest Biscuit Ale. I followed the same routine, cursed Burt and so on, but when I tasted the beer just before bottling again there was something not right about it. I'd been brewing long enough to know that it wasn't how it should be, and this was the second batch that didn't taste right to me. There was a sourness again, not as pronounced as the blonde, but not quite right. Something potentially very serious was happening. Was the beer getting contaminated? Was it the new process I was using with the chilling unit? It was impossible to know, but clearly something needed to be done, so what I did was I just ignored all my gut feelings and all the evidence in front of me, recited my mantra again and again until I had reached a state of perfect idiocy, then I pretended everything was fine and bottled it anyway.

'It's different from the normal one,' commented Rose a few days later as she tried not to purse her lips. 'It's drinkable.' It was drinkable, I suppose, but barely. And finally the killer blow.

'Is it the blonde beer?' Yes, yes it was the blonde beer, but she was right to question it, because it didn't taste like my usual blonde beer. It had had a week in the bottle and it hadn't improved. It wasn't finished yet. Normally it's two to three weeks before it's ready, but after a week some fermentation should have taken place and therefore it should have a decent amount of carbonation and be getting close to the finished article. This beer was completely flat and cloudy and it tasted undeniably sour.

'It's only been a week in the bottle, so it needs more time to develop the bubbles,' I lied. It should have had at least something by now. I coughed and leaned on the kitchen table. In the last few days I'd developed a heavy cough, and a cold too. There was a darkness coming. I could sense it and I was doing my best to ignore it. It was serious, though. It had implications. I knew that.

'Tommy we're doing the *vendange* on Thursday. Do you want to come?' said Imre. The *vendange* is the harvest of the grapes to make wine that happens in September.

'Yeah, definitely. Sounds brilliant. My parents are staying with us at the moment. Can I bring my mum and dad?'

'Of course you can. The more hands the better.'

I covered the phone and whispered to Dad, 'They're doing a *vendange*. You want to come?' Dad shook his head violently.

'He'd love to come,' I confirmed.

Imre is a young winemaker who moved here from Hungary with his wife Ellie. I think I first met Ellie at the market and we got chatting, and that's how we know them. Imre had rented a parcel of vines near Chinon to make some wine. Now it was ready to be picked.

Vendange sounded great to me: Being pushed around in a wheelbarrow in the sun making daisy chains, working up power-ballad lyrics, occasionally picking grapes from the tumbling bunches that hung from marble pillars – one for me, one for the basket, etc. Wearing flares, listening to Bob Dylan before he went acoustic, smoking doobies, not wearing a bra, it sounded brilliant.

'The *vendange* is hell,' said my father.

'Braless. Sounds all right to me,' I replied.

*

Lots of vineyards use a grape-picking machine to do the *vendange* nowadays. Imagine a cross between a tractor and a mechanical everyday park flasher. It has large, thin legs on tractor wheels that straddle the row of vines, passes the individual vines between them, through the flaps of its rain mac, and as they pass through, something under its flaps sort of tickles the grapes off. It gently deflowers them. I dare not think what might be under its flaps. It's really creepy. It plucks the grapes from the branches, leaving the rest of the vine, leaves and all intact, if slightly violated.

Some producers will still hand-pick grapes. You can have more control over the quality of grapes if you hand-pick them, so the really good wines are often hand-picked. Also, if you're a small producer, you might hand-pick them as well, because you don't have a mechanical picker.

A week on, and when we gathered under the shade of a large oak tree in the middle of the vineyard for croissants that morning, an unusually hot Thursday morning in September, I assumed it was a selection of Imre and Ellie's friends he'd pulled together. But now, thinking back, it was probably mostly people serving a community-service sentence. I was still in good spirits, although my mother and father were unusually quiet. Imre gave us a quick talk on what he wanted – he was making a high-quality Chinon wine with Cabernet Franc grapes, so he only wanted the high-quality grapes, not grapes that had shrivelled. I didn't pay much attention. I had earmarked a spacious wheelbarrow to sit in and was soliciting for a wheelbarrow pusher when suddenly Imre handed me a bucket and secateurs and assigned me a row. Before I knew it, everyone was picking grapes with determination. It was back-breaking, unending labour, and because no one else was slacking off, it would be very obvious if I did, so I was forced to work flat out.

'Imre, how much of the vineyard is yours?' I said as I wilted against an uncomfortable vine.

'Up to the tree in that direction and to the road in that direction,' said Imre with a grin, pointing to the horizon.

'Oh my God. Then it's true. This will never end,' I said. And I realised then, all too late, that my father was right. The *vendange* was hell.

Hours later, hours of scuttling up and down rows of vines, searching for the cursed grapes and just before I was about to collapse, lunch arrived. Imre provided us with sparkling wine, which I drank like one eats an oyster. Then it was back to work in the heat. By the end I was broken.

The great thing about the *vendange* and what makes it almost worthwhile is the meal at the end of it. Ellie and Imre invited us all back to theirs for what looked like a spectacular feast. They had whole tables dedicated to wine bottles. Unfortunately, by the time starters had been served, I was getting the hurry-up from Rose, so I had to get home to do bedtime for Albert. I dragged my poor mother and father away from the dinner table.

'The *vendange* is hell,' said my father.

I remember camping on the Île de Ré once, and watching the family next to us laying out their table for breakfast. It left a mark on me. They did it every day, the same thing. It was a carefully orchestrated, ritualistic affair, with *viennoiseries*, loaves of bread and pots of jam. One of the men would go down to the bar and come back with two large jugs of chocolate milk. There were cold meats and cheese.

114

The way they laid it all out, they gave breakfast so much respect that it was really quite touching. And yet every day they did it wrong, for every day, despite all this work, they didn't have bacon.

When French people tell me about their trips to the UK or their sons and daughters who work in the UK, they will often declare our food terrible with one exception – the full English breakfast. I see their eyes mist up when they reminisce about breakfast in a Holiday Inn on a work trip to Wigan or in a bed and breakfast in Aberdeen. They love fried breakfasts. Of course they do – we all love fried breakfasts. It's the ace in the pack. They don't cook them over here. They have a fear of them. It's why I'm starting a support group – 'Embrace the Grease' (good album name).

My Aunt Myra sometimes sends me care packages of bacon from G. H. Porter Provisions in Newark, Nottinghamshire. Triple-smoked is best. You can set off smoke alarms just by opening the packet. There's so much to like about the French breakfast, but it's not got that weight that a fry-up has, both figuratively and literally. It doesn't bring you face to face with your own mortality the way a piece of fried bread does. The full English breakfast is a perfect unit – I wouldn't change it, but that doesn't mean we can't add to it, does it? We can still take the lessons we've learned from French breakfasts and garnish the full English breakfast with Gallic trinkets. Every now and then, when the moon is in the third quarter, I have started eating the Apex breakfast.

Apex Breakfast

Ingredients

- Toulouse sausages – big fat ones
- Butter (for almost everything)
- Sensible British sausages
- Lamb merguez sausages (say what?) from Adrien the shepherd
- Mushrooms, sliced
- Triple-smoked bacon from G. H. Porter provisions
- Eggs from the garden
- Monseur Richard's *coeur de boeuf* tomatoes, sliced
- Worcester sauce
- French bread (for frying and for butter and apricot jam)
- Heinz baked beans
- Croissants, *pain tradition* and *pains au chocolat*, preferably from the bakery Subileau
- Coffee
- Hot chocolate
- Apricot juice
- Apricot jam
- Charcuterie
- Sliced cheeses
- A ten-litre box of Fred's red

I was joking about the ten-litre box of Fred's red. You shouldn't drink red wine with breakfast. You'll need a few bottles of Fred's fizz.

Method

Before you do anything, pour yourself a glass of Fred's fizz. Pour it up to the rim. DO NOT mix it with orange juice. Fizz mixed with orange juice is revolting. Also, DO NOT eat anything before your first glass of fizz. The body absorbs alcohol with the utmost gumption on an empty stomach, and with the addition of fizz, you can be drunk as a lonely pirate within seconds.

Now, you'll need a dedicated sausage pan for this. For future reference, any recipe that starts with 'You'll need a dedicated sausage pan' is a winner. Start with the Toulouse sausages because they're the fattest. Toulouse sausages are made with red wine and garlic. There's always room for a sausage made with red wine and garlic. Put them in a frying pan with some butter. After you've finished your first glass of fizz, add the British sausages and after your second glass of fizz add the merguez sausages. Merguez sausages originate from North Africa. They are traditionally made with lamb and are spicy. There's always room for a spicy sausage. While they are cooking, you need to get the sliced mushrooms frying in more butter. When the sausages are nearly done (around four glasses of fizz), cook the bacon in a separate frying pan on a medium heat – hot enough to render the fat. Push the bacon rind into the hot fat with a fork to really get it crispy. The more care and attention you pay the bacon, the better your life will be.

Once done (approx. two glasses of fizz), remove the bacon and fry the eggs. Chuck the tomatoes into the pan as well. Add some Worcester sauce to the mushrooms.

Finally, when everything is done, add some more butter to all the pans and scatter them with slices of bread. Fry the bread until crispy (approx. one and a half glasses of Fred's fizz). Plate up and then surround the plate with an orbit of croissants, *pains au chocolat*, slices of *pain tradition* spread with apricot jam, cold meats and sliced cheeses. Line up a strong coffee, a good hot chocolate (try the brand Monbana), a half pint of apricot juice and a chilled bottle of Fred's fizz. Take the rest of the day off.

CHAPTER 7

I burst through the door.

'Rose, I've got some terrible news!'

Rose was nowhere to be seen. Instead, Gadget the grumpy miniature horse was standing in the middle of our kitchen eating his breakfast from the counter. He looked up at me and seethed. He didn't need to say anything. I'd forgotten I wasn't allowed in the house.

'Ah. Right. Sorry, Gadget,' I said as I backed out slowly.

Once in the garden a thought occurred to me. *Isn't it Gadget that's not supposed to be in the house?*

I burst through the door.

'Gadget, what the titting hell are you doing in here? Get out!'

Gadget groaned, yawned at me and slinked out, swatting me with his tail as he passed by. In came Rose from the living room to see what the fuss was about.

'Rose, I've got some terrible news,' I repeated.

'Why are there hoof marks in the kitchen?' she enquired.

'Never mind that. I just ran over Burt in the drive.'

'Oh my God. Is he dead? We'll get him to the vet's in Saint-Gervais-les-Trois-Clochers. It might not be too late.' Rose began to put her shoes on.

'No, I don't think you understand.'

'Put Albie and Margot in the car. We'll put Burt in the boot. Is he breathing?' Rose continued.

'Wait, no, stop, Rose. There's no need to go to the vet's.'

'He's already dead? You killed him. The poor little thing.'

'But that's just it, Rose. That's not the terrible news.'

'What?'

'He's perfectly fine. That's what I'm trying to tell you.'

'He's fine? But you ran him over. What's—'

'Yes, I ran him over all right. He should be well dead, but this is the thing – there's not a scratch on him. Not a scratch, Rose. He's out there right now, chewing my wallet. I don't know how he got my wallet. He must have pickpocketed me when I was checking his pulse, but the point is, he's immortal, Rose. He's immortal! Don't you see? He's the hound of Beelzebub. That's the terrible news. There can be no doubt now. We find ourselves preparing for the final battle of good versus evil. He's here to end us, Rose. It's Armageddon. It's coming.'

I looked out of the door into our garden to see Burt weeing on my National Insurance card.

'FOR CRYING OUT LOUD, BURT! DESIST!' I shouted.

'Oh, for Christ's sake Tommy. He's just a dog.'

'That's what they said about Hitler.'

'Nobody said that about Hitler.' We stood in silence for a moment. I knew Rose wouldn't treat this with the gravity it deserved. I watched Burt in the garden for the rest of the day to see if he showed any delayed symptoms of trauma. He seemed absolutely fine. And yet there was something about him. Something was changing before my eyes.

*

By the end of October the darkness had arrived. I was still ill. I'd been ill pretty much since the beer had been going bad. It had started with a cough – a real rasper, lungs of sandpaper – that gradually moved up the throat, resided for an Indian summer in the tonsils, where it spent its time creating an ocean of bright-green snot, before moving to the sinuses and opening the floodgates. This lasted for weeks. Finally it moved into my ear, which consequently had become completely deaf. I had the viral equivalent of a terrorist cell being hunted around my respiratory system by determined, well-backed antibodies that had finally cornered it in my ear, where it had still somehow managed to obliterate my sense of taste. Except that whereas that should have been the end of it, I was now starting to cough again. It had slipped through the net and we were back to square one. This didn't surprise me in the least, because at this moment in time I had completely run out of luck. I was in negative luck. So many times in the last few weeks I thought we'd reached the nadir, only for things to get worse. Finally, I realised there was no nadir.

Everything had fallen apart so quickly. We were doing so well – orders from supermarkets, orders from Patrick the distributor – it had all fallen into place and then the beer just stopped coming out properly. I thought it must be a bacterial contamination. The way to get rid of a bacterial contamination is to clean, so that's what I did. Every time I cleaned the brewery and brewed again, I thought the problem had been solved. The beer would ferment well; initially it would seem to taste OK out of the fermenter. But it wouldn't finish fermenting. That was the sign. Normally, once the fermentation is over, the airlock on the top of the fermenter stops bubbling because no more gasses are being

121

produced. But these beers, once the vigorous fermentation had finished, would continue to bubble very gently, seemingly indefinitely. Something else was going on in that fermenter. And then I would taste the beer after a couple of weeks and there'd be an ever-so-slight sourness. It was so slight that, along with the fact that I could hardly taste anything because of this cold, and sourness and bitterness at low levels can be quite hard to distinguish between, I could convince myself that the beer might be all right and I was so desperate for it to be all right. So I'd add a little sugar and yeast and bottle it and then in the bottle it would get worse.

In some cases the beer wouldn't re-ferment in the bottle at all, and in other cases it would develop much more sourness and off notes as it re-fermented. Either way, despite the fact it was perfectly OK to drink, it was unsellable, because it tasted horrible. And each time a brew failed, I became more desperate, because now I had orders to fill, I could see the doorway to an easy (easier) life, and suddenly it was starting to close. For each brew that went wrong, it was even more important that the next one came out OK, so when I tried the next one, I convinced myself it was OK, but it wasn't. It was off, time and time again.

And so thousands of pounds worth of crap beer began to stack up in my brewery. Months and months of work, expensive hops, literally tonnes of malt was going to go down the drain. A mountain of unsellable bottles. An unmissable monument to my failure.

At the same time both of our cars developed problems. I wouldn't be surprised if they'd caught the same virus I had. It would be expensive to fix them, so instead we continued to drive them. They limped and coughed round Richelieu as people stared. Then one of the pumps in my brewery broke. Poitou Bobinage (*If a man cleaning valves makes you renege on your vows, come to Poitou Bobinage!*) said they could fix it again, but it wouldn't last much longer. I had to buy a new pump. That was €500. All the money from the summer had gone.

To top it all, there'd been an almighty battle in the barn where I store my malt. The result was that Marple the cat, in valiantly defending the honour of the Barnes household, had chewed a rat clean in half, but she hadn't been left unscathed. She'd taken a bite to the cheek that had become infected and had to be treated by the vet. Vets are expensive, but I was happy to pay for her to get patched up. Apart from Louis, and Bella the Cameroonian sheep, she was pretty much the only animal we had that wasn't a complete arsehole. They put her in a collar for a week while the stitches were in. The day before the stiches were due to be removed, Marple escaped from her collar and scratched out all her stitches, so they had to restitch her. *Vets are really expensive*, I thought. A week later, the day before the second vet's appointment, she escaped from her collar again and scratched out all the stitches. *Vets are really expensive and maybe Marple is an arsehole*, I thought. And all the while I felt so ill. Snot poured from my nose constantly. Tired, listless, I dragged myself round the brewery, barely getting the minimum done at a time when I needed more energy than ever to get the brewery back on track.

Margot was one year old in October. She'd been walking since she was nine months old. She was nuts. The thing about Margot was that she was absolutely intent on daredevilry. Albert, our first child, is actually reasonably sensible, on reflection. But Margot thrived on the look of fear in our eyes when she balanced on the edge of a wall or she threw herself at a nest of wasps. The kid was mad. We'd have to watch her all the time. Albert started calling me a dirty snail and Margot would punch me in the stomach at any opportunity. Then Margot caught the same bug that I had, which was unsurprising because everywhere I went a trail of snotty tissues followed me. She began waking up again every hour or two in the night because she couldn't breathe well.

Bills rained in. Electricity, car insurance, customs and excise, taxes we'd never heard of. Bottle suppliers fed up with waiting months for their bills to be paid were starting to get heavy. Label printers too. I'd long run out of stock. Well, I mean I had thousands and thousands of bottles of beer, but I couldn't sell any of them. I put off Patrick the beer distributor for as long as I could, but eventually he lost interest. Likewise the hypermarché in Chinon. Soon all my big orders had disappeared into thin air. I desperately needed to make some beer I could sell. And with my big contracts gone, I had no choice but to go back to selling it at fêtes and markets as quickly as I could. In what seemed like an instant, the door to an easier life had firmly shut.

I brewed again in the bleak autumn, but the beer came out sour. I didn't even bottle it. I knew after a few days in the fermenters that it was shit. It's hard to sell much beer in October anyway if your main market is fêtes, but I didn't have any beer to sell at all. We had nothing, and I urgently needed to start brewing for the Christmas markets. I'd realised after last year's Christmas markets that what I needed to do was make a Christmas beer. Two Christmas beers, even. Make gift packs. Wrap things up. And I'd had an idea for a brilliant Christmas beer – a Christmas pudding stout! It felt like it would work to me. There's a malt called Special B that gives a raisin-like flavour; I would add traditional Christmas pudding spices – nutmeg and cinnamon – and I would finish by adding dried orange peel. I knew if I did this, I would do well at the Christmas markets, but I needed to brew the Christmas beers straight away so they'd be ready, and my beer was just getting worse and worse.

Watching the dream untethering and drifting away and finding you can't do anything about it, you can't seem to reach and pull it back, that's an awful feeling. I'll tell you a worse feeling, though. When you realise there's nothing to replace it. You haven't got a Plan B. That's when it feels like your insides are getting sucked down into the ground. That's when you stop sleeping, when you stop noticing anything beautiful, anything enjoyable. When this brewery went tits to the wind, and it was well on its way to going tits to the wind, there was nothing else behind it.

I was out of my depth. I didn't know enough about brewing beer. I had finally been exposed as a fraud, as I knew I always would be. What was I doing? I was like a second-rate racing-car driver – if the car was working fine I could steer it round the bends, but if it broke down I didn't have the knowledge to fix it. I could only drive the thing. And this car had fundamentally broken down.

Rose booked us a week in a fisherman's cottage in Saint-Martin-de-Ré on the Île de Ré, off the west coast of France near La Rochelle. It was a town of tiny cobbled streets and single-storey whitewashed houses with terracotta tiles. Seafood and salt crystals everywhere you looked. A medieval fortified harbour scattered with tables and chairs tumbling out of the cafés and restaurants, as fishing boats puttered in and out of the harbour in the light October sunshine. Overflowing bowls of mussels. Circles of oysters around dishes of chopped shallot vinaigrette. It's a paradise over there on the Île de Ré. I didn't enjoy any of it. I couldn't. I hadn't told Rose how bad the situation with the brewery was. I should have told her that the last thing we could afford was a holiday, but I couldn't bring myself to tell her, because everyone needed to get out of that house.

I wonder what I was like to live with then? Preoccupied, I think. I don't think I was angry, but Rose must have known I wasn't really present. God, I'd love to go back and do that holiday again and enjoy it. Instead I spent the week wincing every time we bought the kids an ice cream and wishing I was back in the brewery. And when the week was over, we got home and I got back into the brewery and I looked at the place and I didn't know what to do.

It was an awful few months. As the autumn ground on, we stopped seeing Damien and Celia. I'm not sure why really, because we used to be such good friends. I think I didn't want people to ask me about the brewery, so perhaps I was avoiding people in general. There was so much going on. Margot didn't sleep. But we didn't seem to see the Bergers any more, save for waving at them if they went past the gate or bumping into them at the market. There was a time when we'd see them every week for *apéros* or a barbecue. Damien had helped me build the brewery. He was a fundamental part of Braslou Bière, and now we barely saw each other, even to say hello to.

I would go to the brewery, and cry as soon as I shut the door. Then I'd sit there waiting till the redness in my eyes had faded before I could go back to the house.

There were two things that kept me going. Obviously there was the love of my family and my responsibility towards them and all that stuff that people wheel out, but there was something else. Possibly something even more profound.

'The thing is, Fred, I'm not sure I can fix it. I don't know where to start. I've told Rose we've got all these orders for beer, and now they've all gone. What am I going to do?'

I'd gone to visit Fred because his new red wine was ready and also I needed some counselling. Fred looked at me sagely. He yawned and reached for another bottle of fizz.

The previous year had been exceptionally hot. There'd been a heatwave for most of the summer, which had meant the grapes were full of sugar. If you're some enormous wine producer like Blossom Hill, then when you make your wine, you stop the fermentation where you want it to ensure the wine is the same strength as it always is. But this is the thing: if you're Fred in his barn making his red wine, you just let it ferment out until it's finished. For Fred this meant that because this was such an exceptional year and there was so much sugar in the grapes, his wine got stronger and stronger and stronger – he stopped counting at 14 per cent. It was unprecedented. By the time it was finished, it was like port. It was the most extraordinary wine I'd ever tasted. It was thick – it clung to the side of the glass. It tasted of plum and liquorice. I bought a ten-litre box of it, and I'm telling you it was that wine that saved me. One glass of it and you were in orbit. No matter how bad things got, I knew I had a glass of Fred's red standing by to save me. OK, we know you shouldn't use alcohol as a crutch. We know that because people keep telling us that. But for me it works, so what are you going to do? Fred's nuclear red was my saviour.

*

Now, several very trendy breweries had brought out sour IPAs – hoppy beers but made with a bit of the bacteria lactobacillus that creates lactic acid in the beer, giving it a slightly sour flavour. Sour flavours are the rage in craft brewing at the moment. Brooklyn Brewery had a particularly nice sour ale, so I decided to throw caution to the wind. I was so inspired by Brooklyn Sour Ale that I decided to brew a sour IPA of my own: Burt's Sour IPA – full of passionfruit, grapefruit and other citrusy notes, with a tang at the end from the lactic acid. That was the official line. The truth was that while the other breweries were deliberately making sour ales, mine wasn't supposed to be sour at all. It was supposed to be my usual IPA, but like the last six brews I had produced, it had gone sour. The last five blonde brews I'd done were undrinkable. They were to be poured down the sink. Effectively €10,000 worth of beer. The Biscuit Ale I'd made was the least affected. I told myself it was OK, but it wasn't OK. It definitely wasn't OK. It was drinkable, but it wasn't right. And the IPA had come out a bit sour, but it was strangely likeable. I'd go further and say that if you like sour beers, it was actually bloody good. Better, in fact, than the Brooklyn Sour Ale. In fact, it was certainly good enough to sell.

The problem was, my market wasn't craft brew enthusiasts, it was the general public and they didn't particularly want a sour beer. If it was one of a range of other beers it would have been fine, but it's like an abstract artist. You can't just jump straight to the weird shit: you have to demonstrate that you are a decent artist in the first place, then you can do the weird shit, and the sour beer on its own without a range of other more conventional beers behind it was just the weird shit. Along with the not-very-good

Biscuit Ale, It was all that I had, though. Still, I signed up to a two-day fête in late October called L'Art et Lard in a village called Le Petit-Pressigny because we were now desperate.

And so it was that I rumbled into Le Petit-Pressigny, a fifty-minute drive in a normal car or an hour and fifteen minutes in the Tub of Thunder (TVNM) to the east of Braslou. As I drove, I could see a spider dangling precariously on the thinnest of threads from the ceiling of the van. Le Petit-Pressigny is a quaint village on the little River Aigronne. It's home of the Michelin-starred Restaurant au Promenade. I wasn't interested in Michelin stars and all that shit; I had a fête to fail at. The van was full of my all-new Burt's Sour IPA and a substandard Biscuit Ale. I shouldn't have gone. It's hard to sell stuff you know is shit. It's humiliating. I regretted it the moment I arrived.

The day went on for ever. I sold hardly any beer, frankly because I didn't really want people to buy it. People who tasted it told me exactly what they thought of it. I rolled home dejected. There was no point going back the next day, I told myself.

And yet, the next morning I was back in the van on my way to Le Petit-Pressigny. The night had been punctuated with screaming children even more than usual, I can't have had more than two hours sleep, but it didn't matter. In fact, it had helped. I'd spent the night cradling my baby Margot in a rocking chair and I felt renewed determination. Something had come back into me. It didn't matter whether I was embarrassed about the beer; it didn't matter whether it was a shameful experience. That was selfishness. The beer would get better eventually, but at this minute the only thing that mattered was I had to sell beer any way I could. I had two children and a wife who had been stuck in a house looking after them for years now. She'd sacrificed her ambitions so I could run around acting like a tit. When I climbed in the van, I felt elated because suddenly all the bullshit was gone. My objective was clear: sell beer – sod everything else. In front of the windscreen the same spider began to haul itself back up towards its web on this most fragile thread. But then up on the telephone wires buzzards stared ominously down at me, looking as if I were prey and I thought to myself, *Come on, guys, conflicting metaphors – you'll confuse the reader.* The coughing engine gradually arrived at a consistent rhythm of combustion and off rolled the Tub of Thunder (the van, not me, for Christ's sake) back into battle.

I'm telling you now, not a person went past my stall that day without having a Braslou Bière thrust in their face. I smiled a manic smile and I talked about absolutely anything to anybody. Some people were upset. Some people were rude. It didn't matter. For that Sunday I was that prick from *The Apprentice* trying to sell artichoke-scented soap bars or whatever they have to do. And I sold beer. I sold and sold. It wasn't the best day at a fête I had ever had, but it was OK. It was humiliating and all those things, there are people that will never buy a Braslou Bière again because it wasn't great beer, but to hell with it; it would keep us going for another week or two. The next job was to work out how to make my brewery work again, but I didn't really know where to start.

CHAPTER 8

This is where it gets weird.

Ever since I'd run Burt over a couple of weeks earlier, something had changed. Something in his demeanour and something in his eyes. My initial fears about this signalling the end of days had faded as, if anything, Burt's temperament had improved. And at another disastrous Richelieu market on a cold November morning after I'd spent hours telling him that the second child was easier than the first, I suddenly realised what had changed and it made sense in a way that you may well find challenging.

'Did you take Burt to the market with you this morning?' asked Rose. I'd settled down at the table and was fixing myself a cheese sandwich with the king of breads – a *pain tradition* from the Subileau bakery.

'You mean Diana?'

'I mean Burt. Our dog Burt.'

'Diana? Yes, I took Diana with me this morning.'

'Right. Why are you calling Burt "Diana"?' I could sense a dread in Rose's voice. She didn't want to know the answer. She would think it was stupid. Childish. Silly. Well, not this time, *Rose.*

'It's fairly straightforward, Rose. You see, I'd noticed something had changed in Burt ever since I ran him over, and today at the market, as I stared into his eyes, it dawned on me what had happened. It's quite difficult to say this, Rose, but, well, Burt has been possessed by Princess Diana. The people's Elton John or whatever she was.'

'Oh, Jesus.'

'Seriously, Rose. Look at his eyes. Her eyes. Ever since I ran her over, she's had these eyes. They're so demure. There's only one person in history who had eyes as demure as that. I'm telling you, it has to be the late princess. I'm quite serious about this, Rose – Burt's been possessed by the ghost of Princess Diana. I know it in my heart. I think the sooner we all come to terms with this, the sooner we can buy her a golden carriage.'

Rose groaned and reluctantly stepped forward to look at Burt/Diana's eyes.

'Tommy, I haven't got time for this rubbish. Margot has a doctor's appointment at four and Albert just did a poo on the – oh my goodness. Is it? It – it can't be.' Rose leaned closer, deftly skirting round Albert's poo on the rug and stared into Burt's eyes. 'It's Princess Diana, as I live and breathe.'

'Told you.'

'Wait a minute. It can't be Diana. Maybe he's just had a stroke.'

'It's Diana. Watch this. Diana. Here Diana.'

Burt/Diana – trotted over and wondered at me with that doe-eyed stare that captivated a nation.

'Was it MI6, Diana?'

I was aware that I might be going mad. I was under pressure. With the brewery going down the pan and the

money running out, I could feel the pressure inside my skull, pressing my brain. I'd never experienced that much pressure. And yet there was Diana. I could see her in my big fat dog. Rose knew it too, although she couldn't admit it. I could tell from her hesitation that she knew it was Diana. And I had this feeling that Princess Diana was here to save me. But how? Why? Find out more in the next chapter of –
Trouble Brewing in the Loire!

CHAPTER 9

We like to lament social media as a breeding place for shitty little arguments that grow and grow and become endless. We talk about this phenomenon as a new thing, but in fact this sort of infinite internet argument has a historical predecessor: Belgium.

Belgium is less of a country and more of a never-ending quarrel. It's various parts of France, Germany and Holland that have been flung together for bad reasons and now they hate each other. It can't be that bad, you say – all countries have their regional quarrels, don't they? Well, a few years ago, Belgium went over 500 days without an elected government because they couldn't agree on one. That is actually a world record. No other country has ever been that unreasonable. What a badge of honour.

It's funny, then, that the Belgians have a reputation for being boring. I think it's because we don't see much of them in the UK, but when you think about it, they make the best beer in the world, the best chips and the best chocolate, so I very much doubt they give a shit what you think. And when you actually meet the Belgians, they prove to be anything but boring. They drive like maniacs. They didn't introduce driving licences in Belgium until the 1960s. They are always the fastest drivers on the road, their white-and-red number plates flashing past you in the fast lane at death-defying speeds. Until fairly recently, obeying traffic lights was optional in Belgium. Somebody told me that and I haven't bothered to research it, but it sounds plausible to me. The Belgians drink hard, smoke, and eat chips and chocolate. They're living the dream.

Benoît is Belgian. He runs the Little Belgique brewery down in Sammarçolles, a thirty-minute drive away, near Loudun. His beers are superb. The British love to drink beer; the Belgians love to make it. I wasn't that aware of Belgian beers when I lived in London. I knew their reputation and I'd tasted a few, but in most supermarkets the selection was small and expensive. But in France, in any supermarket, Belgian beers dominated the beer section and they are cheap. Two euros a bottle or less for beers that I'd heard beer lovers in the UK talk about in hushed tones. And they are something else, Belgian beers. They're normally strong – 8 per cent and more – but they rarely give this away in their drinking. They are all impeccably made. I've never had a Belgian beer that had any flavours it wasn't supposed to have. At first glance, a lot of their beers seem straightforward, but they aren't. They use spices – coriander, cloves, they use anything they like – but always in the correct quantities, so that it doesn't overwhelm the beer. For example, it's rare to have a Belgian beer that tastes directly of coriander, but that doesn't mean it doesn't have coriander in it and that it hasn't given something to the flavour. There's a huge variety of Belgian beers, from sweet blondes like Leffe to much more bitter beers. But the bitter beers never taste overwhelmingly bitter. They do it all – dark

135

beers, light beers, they use every grain you can imagine, and they trick you into thinking it's simple. In terms of their craft, they're unbeatable. They can't make an IPA, though. I've tried several IPAs from big Belgian breweries, and they can't seem to resist using a Belgian yeast or an odd selection of hops. They're very drinkable, but they're not IPAs. I've just realised that I bang on about how I hate people trying to define beers and here I am going full beer Nazi on the Belgians. I take it all back.

I knew there was another brewery about half an hour away pretty much since I started selling beer, but we'd never really crossed paths until I visited them the year before in 2018. That time Benoît wasn't in, but I sat drinking their beer with his sister, and the beers were fantastic. He had a brewery about the size of mine in an outbuilding, but it was streets ahead in terms of the layout, cleanliness and technology. Benoît makes what at first I thought were traditional Belgian beers, but as I got to know him, I realised they're not all that traditional. Some are made with yeasts that aren't necessarily traditional Belgian yeasts and a variety of modern hops from around the world. He uses what he thinks will make the best beer. He doesn't make IPAs or stouts or anything like that. He makes four or five really good, really well-made, perfectly balanced Belgianish beers. And, when you think about it, he's just following Belgian tradition. Belgian beers have always been made using the best ingredients they could get and the best processes. If that means taking ingredients and ideas from other countries, then fine. There are some Belgian beers that claim to be traditional, of course, such as the Abbaye beers that have been brewed for hundreds of years by monks, although I suspect a lot of the more commercial ones are using new varieties of hops now, and they're certainly using modern processes, but generally in Belgium you get the feeling that anything goes in pursuit of a better beer.

I'd always assumed that Belgian beers followed some long line of tradition, but in fact a lot of Belgian brewing was wiped out after the French Revolution, when they forced the abbeys to close, and it was really only taken up again in the early twentieth century where, to some extent, they started afresh. Some traditions must have continued, some recipes rediscovered, but a lot of what we think of as traditional Belgian beer is only a century or so old. I suppose that's why they're not that sentimental about brewing traditions.

It's not only the Belgians who aren't sentimental. For something that feels so country-specific and traditional, like beer, it's interesting to find out that brewers in Europe and indeed the world have always been innovative and interested in different ingredients. The history of brewing is littered with examples of countries taking hops, malts and technology from each other in order to make better beer. Citra, arguably the most popular hop in the craft beer world, a hop developed in America that has transformed the flavour profiles of new beers, has in its lineage traditional hops from both Germany and the UK. Where was I? Ah yes. Benoît.

Benoît and I drank beer in my driveway next to my van. As a brewer, if another brewer comes round, you must drink beer with them. It's a law of physics. I don't know if other trades do the same. If two plumbers meet up, do they clear a U-bend? I'd be interested to know. Benoît had come over to mine to borrow my malt mill because his had broken down and he needed to brew. Benoît is a slim, tall, fair-haired, lived-in man with sensible, pale blue eyes, brows that imply forgiveness and a soft, growling voice, and he's normally to be found resignedly smoking a cigarette. He has a permanent look of sympathy on his face, although maybe that's just when he meets me. He speaks quickly and affably, which makes him difficult to understand, but he always finishes with a joke, so I know to laugh at the end. He knows a million times more than I do about brewing and he's very open and he will help wherever he can. I have never experienced any animosity from other brewers. I've never met another brewer who has been anything other than helpful and kind. Why can't we all be like the brewers, guys? As he was leaving with my malt mill he said: 'Everything all right at the moment?'

'Oh yeah. You know. A couple of little things with the brewery,' I replied.

'I tried your sour IPA over at Bruno's bar. It was very nice.'

'Thanks, Benoît. It's made with Callista hops, but I just thought it needed something else, you know, so I soured it.' I fibbed.

'OK. Hey, thanks for the mill. I'll bring it back next week. Oh, and by the way, if you have a contamination in the brewery, it's almost always the heat exchanger,' he said with a wink as he got in his car. He knew. He knew that beer was a fluke. He knew what was going on in my brewery and even though I was too proud to tell him the real depths of it, he'd given me the clue I needed and the more I thought about it, the more the shame fell away and the more excited I became. Because Benoît is the type of guy who doesn't just say things for the sake of offering an opinion. If he says something, then it's because he knows. The heat exchanger! Clean the heat exchanger! A last hope!

This could be it. If I could get the brewery going again, then I could still brew beer in time for Christmas.

I bought some new cleaning products and in the next week I cleaned the heat exchanger thoroughly. I gave it an acid wash – where you fill it up with diluted acid to kill any bacteria, and then I brewed. I brewed my Berger Blonde beer in the big fermenter and I brewed two Christmas beers – a spiced amber beer and a Christmas pudding stout – in my smaller fermenters.

I'd put some thought into the Christmas pudding stout, but the amber spiced beer was an afterthought, really. Perhaps the Christmas pudding stout wouldn't appeal to everyone, so I decided to make something a little more recognisable to the French as a second option. I made it with a lot of crystal malt, a malt that gives flavours of caramel and sweetness to the beer. I spiced it with cinnamon and a little orange peel. Less than the Christmas pudding stout. I added some white sugar to get the alcohol up to around 7 per cent. Christmas beers, in my opinion, should help you to forget the horrors of Christmas. If I did it again, I would use less crystal malt and instead of everyday white sugar I would use candied brown sugar. I'm increasingly realising that the type and amount of sugar you use in Belgian beers is crucial.

'The cat is staring at me like crazy. What the hell is her problem?' I was in the living room talking to myself as Marple the cat sat on the stairs. 'There's something in her eyes. Something familiar. Holy shit. Rose, come and see this. ROSE! IT'S JILL SHITTING DANDO IN THE CAT! ROSE! THE CAT IS POSESSED BY JILL DANDO!'

139

Rose ran into the living room.

'It's Jill Dando. I swear it.'

Rose scrutinised the cat for a moment. 'For God's sake, Tommy. That is not Jill Dando.'

'But look at the eyes, Rose. And think about it. She's passionate about fighting crime.'

'She's not passionate about fighting crime. She's a cat.'

'She guards my malt, Rose. She tracks and kills any mice or rats that try and steal it, just like Jill Dando did on *Crimewatch*.'

'You've never seen *Crimewatch*, have you.'

'I'm looking at it right now, Rose. In the flesh. In the shape of a cat.'

'OK, I'm going now. Oh, and what the hell are you listening to? Who's Paul Burrell?'

'Alexa, stop,' I said hastily. 'It's just a book on Audible.'

I'd been trying to discover more about Princess Diana. I wanted to know what she was all about – her hopes, her fears – to try and gain an insight into why she was here, in Burt, so I'd downloaded *A Royal Duty* by Paul Burrell, her former butler. I'll tell you what, though, there are some terribly written books out there (shut the hell up), but that book on Diana – hours of my life I listened to it, eighteen hours of smugness. Oh, the smugness. It was physically painful, but I stuck at it. I'm not shitting you, It's one of the hardest things I've ever done, listening to that book, but it would be worth it. The things I learned. The riches. It's interesting, though, one thing I discovered about Princess Diana since she inhabited my hound that Paul Burrell doesn't tell you – she loves croissants. Adores them.

'Look, Jill. There's something not right in that brewery. I don't know what it is, but I need your help. Have a snoop around. See what you can discover. Report back to me in the morning.'

The next day Jill Dando the cat came in.

'Anything?'

Jill wasn't talking. She was a cat. But I could tell she was trying to get some kind of message across.

'OK, let's go over to the brewery together. You can go and sit on whatever is causing the problems.' Jill agreed in the sense that she didn't say anything because she was a cat. I picked her up and strolled out across the garden to the brewery. I set her down on the dirty concrete floor.

'*Allez go.*' French people say that.

Jill Dando arched her back, stretched out her paws and began to tour the brewery, sniffing boxes, rubbing against the mash tun. She went straight past the chiller. She didn't stop at the fermenters, she circled all the way round and sat down on my feet, staring at me.

'You're the problem,' Jill Dando said.

'Well, obviously. I know that. In the grand scheme of things, yes. But's what's the specific problem?'

Jill Dando didn't answer. She walked into the garden and climbed a tree.

'Oh, for Christ's sake, Jill Dando.'

'Ah crap. It's no good Jill Dando. It's sour.'

It was better than the previous blonde: it was drinkable, but it wasn't right. The deep clean of the heat exchanger hadn't worked. All was lost. The new blonde was still a bit sour straight from the fermenter. It was to go straight down the drain. I still had two fermenters to test, but I was dejected. Reluctantly, I tested the Christmas pudding stout.

'You know what, Jill Dando, that might be OK!' I startled

myself. It was a weird beer, actually. It hadn't come out the way I wanted it to. It had too much cinnamon and nutmeg in. And it had a tartness, but that might have been coming from the orange peel that was in there. It was difficult to tell. But it didn't taste that bad. I had my doubts about it, but with all the spices and the dark malts in it, if there were off flavours, they were being hidden. The problem is, if you've been tasting nothing but off beers for months, it becomes hard to remember what a well-made beer should taste like. Your mind plays tricks with you. Sourness and bitterness become confused. Your desperation for a decent beer clouds your judgement.

Nervous, I tried a sample from the final fermenter – the spiced amber ale.

'Shit. SHIT! It's clean, Jill Dando! It's clean! Jill Dando? Where have you gone, Jill Dando?' Jill Dando the cat had wandered off without me realising.

'It's clean!' I said to myself. Because it was clean. Generally, if a beer is well made, whether you like the actual flavour of the beer or not, it will taste clean. This doesn't apply to lambic beers and other beers where they are looking for sourness and the like, but for your everyday beers, once you know all the flavours you don't want in the beer (and I was now an expert in those flavours), a beer without them tastes clean. There's no other way to describe it. You can have two wildly different beers, but if they are both well made, they'll both have this clean quality to them. I was overjoyed.

I tipped the blonde beer down the drain, but for the first time in months I got my bottling gear prepped and I bottled both the Christmas pudding stout and the amber ale just in time for the Christmas markets. There was no time to lose.

*

I didn't sell much at Lencloître. I turned up to the town square in the van at 7 a.m. on a freezing-cold December morning, because most markets like you to be there at that sort of time to set up. I'm almost always late to markets, so I made sure to get there early because I was a newbie and I wanted to make sure I got a stall. The place was deserted. I sat freezing in the van for an hour and a half before anyone else turned up. It didn't matter, though. When it came to turning up at the wrong time, they'd broken me long before.

As a British person, you can never arrive on time in France. They have whole ministries devising ways to stop the British arriving at the correct time, be that for a restaurant, or *apéros* with the neighbours, or shops, or meetings with bank managers, they will find a way for you to be much too early or embarrassingly late. There must be a hidden-camera TV show in France dedicated to watching the British turn up to shops to find them shut. The disappointment, the rage, the sheer incomprehension on their faces. I would watch that. Because to work out the published opening hours of French shops and restaurants, you need an Enigma machine. Some are shut on Mondays, some do half-days on Wednesdays. Sundays they almost all completely shut, but not all of them, because they don't want you to have any concrete rule to cling to. The actual hours themselves, Jesus. Most places have a two-hour lunch break, so you can forget everything between 12 and 2 p.m. Except not all of them, of course. Then there's some that open from 8.30 to 11.30, then reopen from 3.30 p.m. to 8 p.m. What are they doing between 11.30 and 3.30? It takes years to come to terms with this, and then that's when they really get you. Just when you are finally beginning to accept the absurd opening hours on an emotional level, just when you have recovered from the breakdown and you can once again hear the birds singing and smell the sweet smell of buttercups, just when you're turning things around, they hit you with this, the shopkeeper's favourite trick. You've spent days studying charts, you've consulted the moon and the stars – you've taken advice from high-ranking officials. Everything you know leads you to believe the shop will be open. You can do no more. It *has* to be open. Now, again I can't prove this because I haven't managed to track down the hidden-camera TV show, but what I believe happens is the shopkeeper waits till you're approaching, then they switch off all the lights, lock the door and put up their secret weapon, something nothing can prepare you for: a sign saying *Fermeture Exceptionelle* – exceptional closure. I mean, for Christ's sake. What on earth are you supposed to do with that? It's checkmate. And the thing is, it's not a *fermeture exceptionelle*, because that sign seems to be up on most shops at least once a week. There's nothing exceptional about it FOR CHRIST'S SAKE! Jesus. *Fermeture* cocking *exceptionelle*.

I'd signed up for three Christmas markets this year – Richelieu, Les Ormes and the truffle market at Marigny-Marmande. But before all of them there was the last fair of the year at Lencloître. The fair at Lencloître, a town in the Vienne half an hour south of Braslou, takes place the first Monday of every month. I'd never tried to sell beer there before, despite it being the biggest market for hundreds of miles. It's famous throughout the region. We'd visited once and it was both remarkable and terrifying.

It was a dreary day in the autumn of 2016. The tight pathways between the stalls were packed. Stallholders shouted. Men and women argued. There was everything imaginable for sale. Live animals – chickens, horses, sheep, ducks. A food stall grilling live eels. Stalls selling nothing but onions that stretch on for miles. It was medieval. There were people there that you would never see anywhere else, you know what I mean? You looked at the people leading donkeys round on ropes, the people propping up the make-shift bar drinking white wine in the morning at €1 a pop, and they were people who live in a different universe – a universe of bare chests, of wooden huts and double-handed broadswords, of days hammering lumps of iron, of the plague and mead and wenches and bows and arrows. Rose was pregnant at the time and she found it so overwhelming we had to leave. I hadn't been back to sell beer there because it was scary. But now we were in desperate straits and I had to sell some beer, so I thought the Lencloître market in December must be a good bet for selling beer, which is why I found myself there huddled in the van on a cold December morning wondering what the hell was going on.

No one ever tells you how things work at these places. There's never anyone to phone. You just have to turn up and find the *placeur* – the guy that decides if and where you can set up a stall. He can be anywhere. *Placeurs* don't like to stay in one place. There'll be cafés they inhabit before the market starts, but only for brief periods of time, and they'll tour most of the cafés, so it's pot luck if you get the right one at the right time. Otherwise they'll walk around the market at random, often having nothing on them to suggest they are the *placeur*, and you just have to try and work them out from their body language. Once you find them, they will look you up and down and gesture you to follow them. You chase after them with a gaggle of other hopeful stallholders (all *placeurs* are exceptionally fast walkers) and as they sprint round the market, they bequeath stalls on people with the flick of a wrist. Stallholders disappear to the left and right as they are assigned a place until there's just a few of you left and things are getting tense. Space is limited. Has it all been a waste of time? Finally, a swish of the hand directed at you, and you have a spot. You go and introduce yourself to the stallholders around you and you retrieve your van and set up your stall in the allotted space. At Lencloître I was shoved out at the end of the market, away from all the action, so that didn't help, but more than that I got the impression that people weren't there to buy beer. They were there to get chain mail and witches' potions. I'm being a twat. But I didn't sell much at Lencloître, to be honest. It wasn't a success. However, by the time Richelieu Christmas market came round the following weekend, I was battle ready. We had learned from the year before. People didn't want beer at Christmas you see. What people wanted was gift packs.

Over the course of that week we'd turned the living room into a factory. Everywhere crates of beer were piled up. Little wicker baskets were being filled with red shredded paper by Albert while I labelled bottles as fast as I could, and Rose assembled them into gift packs with a Braslou Bière glass in each one. They were wrapped in cellophane and tied with ribbons. We worked mostly in silence like Resistance fighters planning a last desperate attack. We knew what it meant if this failed.

Like the year before, it was raining as I set up at the Christmas market in Richelieu in the mid-morning. It wasn't the same rain as last year, though. It wasn't freezing rain. There was hope. The weather forecast was mixed. If we got lucky, we'd have a few dry spells each day and that might be enough to get the people out of their houses. There was definitely hope. I set up the stand with a table-cloth, with fairy lights all around the stall and I began laying out all the gift packs and I set up my beer pump at the back. It was a triple threat – beer on tap, beers in bottles and gift packs for Christmas presents. It stopped raining in the early afternoon.

'How did it go?' asked Rose as I staggered through the door at quarter to midnight.

'We're going to need more gift packs,' I said. The people of Richelieu had spoken and it turns out they wanted bottles of beer in baskets wrapped in cellophane. I couldn't believe how well we'd sold. It had been a success. We spent the night making up more gift packs.

The next day it rained again, but we had a window of two hours and the same thing happened. We sold all the gift packs. Not only that, people were stopping to try the Christmas beer on tap. It was difficult to compete with the mulled wine stalls, because on a cold afternoon in December some people aren't desperate to drink even colder beer, but there were enough people who did.

'What are they doing?' asked Rose.

'I think it's the Lambada. It's hard to say definitively.'

An impromptu dance had broken out in the stables at the Christmas market in Les Ormes. I love the Christmas market at Les Ormes. I love the people of Les Ormes. The year before, the market had saved my life. This year was even better. The stand next to me sold Caribbean fish frit-ters and rum punch. The stand the other side to me sold cured meats and also rum punch. In between them I was selling my amber ale and Christmas pudding stout on tap.

They were both around 7 or 8 per cent vol. I'd made friends from last year at Les Ormes and they all turned up to drink. They would alternate between the rum-punch stands and my beer. It didn't matter how strong the beer was to them – they drank it all. By the time Rose turned up with the kids, it was like a festival. The entire place was shitfaced. I had ran out of kegs by mid-afternoon, so I was opening bottles to fill people's glasses.

The truffle market in Marigny-Marmande was also a success. The Christmas markets had given us a temporary reprieve. I managed to pay off a few bills and we had enough to buy the kids Christmas presents. We would limp on, but unless I could get all my fermenters making good beer, we wouldn't be able to make enough beer to survive.

I had one 200-litre fermenter that the spiced amber beer had come out of that was working well, one 200-litre fermenter that the Christmas pudding stout had come out of that was all right, although I had my suspicions about it, and the big fermenter still wasn't working properly. The cleaning of the heat exchanger had gone some way to fixing the brewery, but there were other problems.

CHAPTER 10

In January 2020 Rose and I started to argue. Not huge, plate-throwing arguments, but bickering. That for us was the same thing, though. We hardly ever argue, so when we do it means something is wrong. It was inevitable with everything going on. It was surprising we'd made it this far without starting to turn on each other. Neither of us were happy. We didn't have much money and although the brewery was starting to turn out the odd good beer again, Christmas was over and the money made had evaporated. We were in the desperate winter months and we were miles behind.

We'd started taking little pot shots at each other. Shitty little comments here and there, which might not seem like much to an outsider, but they were just the portion of the iceberg that was above sea level.

Rose had just come back from visiting her mum in Padstow, Cornwall. There were always arguments when she came back from Cornwall.

'I'm worried about how you're running the brewery, Tommy. I can help, you know.'

'Thanks for the concern, Rose, but I don't need help. I'm perfectly capable of running my own brewery.'

'Maybe you should be making a beer like Kronenbourg, though. That's what everyone drinks round here.'

'Kronenbourg? OK, Rose.' I was too pathetic to say what I thought, so instead I agreed with her in a way that meant I didn't agree with her.

'And you need to clean it more. It's a mess in there, Tommy. You can't bring people to the brewery and expect them to buy beer.'

'It's my brewery, Rose. I know it's a mess and I am in the process of tidying it, but there's a million other things to do.'

'But it's not earning us any money, Tommy.'

'It will earn us money if you let me get on with it.'

'Fine.' Rose was annoyed. 'Tommy, what do you think about Cornwall?'

'I don't have time to think about Cornwall.' I stomped out of the kitchen and over to the brewery to be on my own.

Rose wanted to get in on the brewery. She had ideas about why it wasn't working; she wanted to get in and clean the brewery down; she thought I should be making different beers, selling in different places. But it was my brewery. So often I get talked out of things, I'm predisposed to accept other people's suggestions ahead of mine, which means my ideas are often pushed to the side or at least diluted. I was aware that that was how I was, so I wanted to defend the brewery at all costs because it was the one thing I had that was really mine and I thought if I started letting other people in, it would soon be theirs and not mine. And I was capable of good ideas – I'd done things that most people wouldn't have done that had proved to be a success. The van I bought, the 1982 Peugeot J9 fireman's van – everyone told me I was mad to get that van, but because it was so unusual and so interesting it had become an icon of the brewery. It was recognised everywhere, as I knew it would be. I mean, yes, I had had obscenities printed across the back of it, but overall it was a masterstroke. There were other things I'd done right. I can't think of them offhand, but I'm pretty sure there were. I'd made a lot of mistakes, but I'd done some good things as well, things I wouldn't have done if I'd let someone else in. But for Rose, she could just see the brewery failing and that impacted on her and the kids, so it was understandable why she wanted to get involved.

There was pressure on every side. It wasn't just the brewery. There was the house. It was starting to fall apart and we couldn't fix it. Gates were rusting, tiles coming off the roof. Sinks leaked, toilets broke.

And then there was Brexit. When you're young it's hard to pinpoint where your anxieties stem from, but as you get older you can begin to identify the causes. For us, we'd had something that had been sitting in our minds slowly dissolving the barriers that keep you sane for two years now and I knew exactly what the root of it was: Brexit. I hate calling it that. Leaving the EU had been weighing our minds since it was announced. Because depending on how it went, we might have to leave France altogether. And it had rumbled on for years.

The not knowing was the thing. How could it drag on like that? How could they let it? These politicians in their townhouses and country piles playing with our lives. They didn't give a shit. They were making tons of money from their hedge funds by humping our country into the ground. It didn't matter to them – the wider economic shit bomb that was about to drop – because Rees-Mogg, that shit, that pin hammer of contempt, wasn't going to get touched by it safely tucked up in his stately home, was he? Or Boris

Johnson – it wasn't going to impact on him shagging his way through the Chelsea cocktail bars like an Old English sheepdog gaffer-taped to a jackhammer, and ultimately that's all that matters to him.

It's the fear of the unknown, isn't it? That's what really causes anxiety. I'm sure psychologists will tell you that, and to have Brexit lingering there for years – something that could be absolutely catastrophic for us – we simply didn't know – all the time just above our heads, a guillotine, it's hard to quantify the damage that was causing us and all the other people like us who were in the same boat. It was too much.

Benoît's brewery was similar to mine in that it was in an out-building next to his house and it was roughly the same size, but it differed in that it was clean. It was so much cleaner than my brewery, immaculate, in fact, and it was well-ordered and you could see a great deal of time and planning had gone into how it was laid out. My brewery was much more natural in the way it had developed and I don't mean natural in a sort of organic, 'nature finds the most effective way' type of deal, I mean natural more in the way a badger always shits in the same a hole. My brewery had become increasingly disgusting. I was constantly having to put traps down for rodents, the floor had two years of spilt beer and yeast caked onto it, and cobwebs hung from the ceiling, so that when the brewery filled with steam they all twinkled from one end to the other like a magical kingdom. Muddy tubes were lying on the floor. The sink had a brown crust on it. I didn't like going into my brewery any more. I felt ashamed of it. I hated brewing in that brewery. It wasn't tenable to continue like that. It was an effort to bring myself to go in because it was such a grim place, and it wasn't right to be brewing beer in such an unsanitary environment. Since the new fermenter and chiller unit had arrived, there was much less space, not just because they took up more space in the brewery, but it meant I was now brewing more beer and that beer stacked up on pallets in the middle of the brewery. I couldn't clean the floor because there was barely any floor left to clean. I realised that I was waiting for the whole thing to rot to the ground.

What is Burt doing on the sofa? Get Burt off the sofa,' said Rose one morning in early February.

'Rose, this is just the sort of persecution Diana faced from the royal family when she split with Prince Charles. Now, we need a stress-free atmosphere. I'm doing some faith healing,' I said.

'Get Burt off the sofa,' insisted Rose.

Diana flopped down from the sofa and waddled off into the kitchen.

'Tommy, I'm worried.'

'Don't worry Rose, MI6 don't know she's here. You haven't told anyone, have you?'

'Not that. Have you read about this coronavirus in China? They reckon they've found an outbreak in Italy now.'

'Nah. We've had this before. SARS and all that. It never amounts to anything,' I said with absolute confidence.

'OK. But I'm also worried we haven't got any money. My bank card got refused today. And I'm worried about you and this Princess Diana business. Are you OK, Tommy? I think you might need to see somebody,' said Rose.

'Don't worry, Rose. I'm fine,' I said.

I could still feel the pressure of everything squeezing against my brain. I was worried too. I was going mad.

When we lived in London I was an aspiring stand-up

comedian at night. I'd been going for maybe four years, but the truth was I didn't have the right make-up for it. On a good night with a good crowd I could soar, but if it was a tricky night with not many people there (and the bottom rungs of stand-up comedy in London are almost always like that), I couldn't turn it around and you can make as many excuses as you want about the crowd and the atmosphere, but the good comedians could turn it around. I had seen them do it. There was a time when I had the confidence to ride those nights out, but I lost it, and once you lose it, it's hard to arrest the slide.

Stand-up had a lasting effect on me. I learned more in those four years about myself and about other people than the previous thirty years. I learned that pressure could make me an arsehole. I saw what other people were like under pressure (mostly arseholes). I learned that you can ignore fear and do the exact opposite of what your instincts are telling you. That there's looking at the pros and cons, there's prevaricating and making excuses, but actually getting up and doing something extinguishes everything else and it's doing things that makes things happen. I learned that you can just do things if you can ignore the fear. Finally, I learned that, ultimately, I was a coward. Because every comedian dies now and then, but it's how you die. There were gigs, awful gigs, gigs in pubs where they were showing the football on the big screen at the same time and the Millwall supporters' club had turned up, gigs where no one did well, but what struck me was that some comedians who had really died somehow came out with their dignity still intact and yet I didn't leave with my dignity intact even when I'd extracted the odd laugh here and there. It was because they showed that they didn't care what the audience thought of them, whereas when things went against me, I started to wilt, out there on stage, in front of everyone. To my shame I wilted, and that stuck with me.

Eventually I failed at stand-up and that really left something on me, because for a while it felt like stand-up comedy might have been the one thing I was going to succeed at. I've not been the same, really. My shell had been cracked. Now I was getting the same feeling with the brewery. After all I'd been through, it was failing and I wasn't sure how another failure was going to affect me. This time the audience was the people we'd met out here, my neighbours, our friends, but the feeling was the same. I was wilting. Oh God, right in front of everyone.

I think I knew that the cat wasn't Jill Dando, and I knew that a dog being possessed by Princess Diana was definitely odd, but with the dog there was something in those eyes. I'm telling you as I sit here tapping away it was Diana.

'I'll move some more money over from my business account. Don't worry, Rose.'

'Why shouldn't I worry, Tommy? What are we going to do?'

'I'm going to go out and get us some new orders. I'll target more shops. We'll be fine.'

'OK, Tommy. You'll tell me if you're not all right, won't you?'

'Don't worry, Rose. We'll be OK. Diana is here to save us,' I didn't say. I just nodded.

The truth was we didn't have any money left. I didn't know what I was going to do. I had an overwhelming feeling that I needed to get out. I needed divine help and for divine help there was only one place I could go.

*

My phone was buzzing in my pocket. It had been buzzing all morning. This time it was Scott.

I decided to answer it. 'Hey, Scott, how's it going?'

'Yeah, fine, how are you?'

'Yeah, good. You know.'

'Rose asked me to call you. She says you're not answering your phone. Where are you?'

'I'm on the speed bump in Marigny-Marmande,' I said.

'OK. How is it up there?'

'It's quite underwhelming, really.' Truth be told, the Marigny-Marmande speed bump suddenly didn't feel nearly as sacred as I'd hoped. I'd been sitting there for a few minutes and it just seemed like a really steep speed bump. I got to thinking about Diana and I remembered her eating the cheese off the coffee table and that gave me another idea. 'Hey, Scott, you want to go to Époisses?'

'To see the cheese? Yeah, definitely.'

'OK. It's a four-hour drive by the way.'

'I know, Tommy.'

'Great. I'll pick you up tomorrow at 6am.'

I'll tell you about Époisses. The French are generally very sniffy about British cuisine, but they're wrong to be. Indeed, British food has moved on a lot since the seventies, and the way we cook now in general is nothing to be ashamed of. In fact, nowadays we have a much wider influence and cook a more varied cuisine than the French. And, certainly, some of our produce has always been of a high standard. But in France cooking and eating and drinking is not something that starts and stops around mealtimes. It's part of everything. It's all one with the flow of life. That made me sound like a tit, but you know what I mean. I'm not saying that no British people talk well about food and drink, so sit back down, foodies. Yes, some of you can describe a Sauvignon blanc in a way that makes everyone else secretly think you're a prick – but the way the French talk about food is so natural. And, unlike in the UK, it's all of them, from Michelin-starred restaurateurs to bus drivers. It's in their DNA. We're simply not like that in the UK.

However, one of the areas where English cuisine stands up to French cuisine is our produce, our cured meats and our cheese. The French won't admit it – in fact, they would find it impossible to comprehend that the English might make cheeses that rival theirs – but the truth is, there are very few French cheeses that can outdo a really good vintage Cheddar. An aged Comté is a great cheese, a marvellous cheese, in fact. Some of the cheeses from the Auvergne are superb, as are the Jura cheeses. If you are into goat's cheese, there isn't anything better than our local cheese – Sainte-Maure de Touraine. None of them are as good as a good English Cheddar. There is, though, one French cheese that even a mighty Cheddar can't beat. The trump card. The reason the French can still reign supreme. That cheese is called Époisses; it originally came from the town of the same name in Burgundy in the east of France and it is incomparable.

It arrives in a quaint little round wooden box, like a hand grenade in My Little Pony wrapping paper, and when you lift the delicate lid it looks benign, a Camembert-esque rind with an orange hue, and then the smell reaches you. And then the drums begin.

At its best it doesn't even resemble cheese. At its best, when it has ripened (it ripens!) so that the middle is soft, it's a terrible, gorgeous, scandalous, orange, alkaline, pulsating slime fruit from Uranus that seeps into every pore in your skin, taints everything it contacts with its outrageous honking odour that hops back and forth over the line between heaven and hell and hypnotises you into forgetting anything you've eaten before it.

At its best you need a spoon to serve it. A spoon! It had better be stainless steel as well, because I'm pretty sure it would dissolve anything else. You have to have red wine with it, or something stronger. Port. Have port with it. They'll tell you to have a dessert wine with it. Ignore them. Have port. It's not like a Cheddar you could have on a sandwich at a picnic in Richmond Park. No, it needs to be eaten at night. Port. Cigars. Tom Waits. Lightning storms. Roofs falling in. Bats flying around your ears.

The first mouthful will disgust you – wafts of bloody battlefields, flavours of prehistoric manure, of scented Viking's crotch, of the insides of a hippopotamus's ear, but now it's too late, because it is already hauling you into a black hole lined with purple leopard-print fur and out through the other side into a world of talking pterodactyls and floating volcanoes. A world that blurs and then comes into vivid focus over and over to the rhythm of your heart, where colours become sounds and sounds become liquids and you're not sure whether you're eating the cheese or the cheese is eating you. You will not care again for the people around you, now shadows darkening into the walls. The only thing is Époisses and you will reside as a prisoner of the Époisses for as long as it desires you.

They'll tell you it is made of cow's milk, but that's because if they told you the truth, that it's made from the milk of great white sharks fed on only the most poisonous reptiles, it would probably not pass strict EU health and safety laws. So, when they tell you it's made of cow's milk, nod politely and give them a wink.

They'll tell you it's washed in *mar*, a sort of rough brandy. This may be true, but it's *mar* that has first been gargled by a satanic monk. So, when they tell you it's washed in *mar*, nod politely and smile a little smile.

They'll tell you it's aged for fifty-six days. They won't tell you they are talking about days on Venus, where each day lasts 5,832 hours. So, when they tell you it's aged for fifty-six days, look to the heavens and laugh a little laugh.

Interestingly, if you join the dots between each of the four *fromageries* that make Époisses on a map, you get a detailed line drawing of Vlad the Impaler riding a mobility scooter. You can pretend its coincidence, if that comforts you.

If the Americans had discovered Époisses, it would be safely locked away in Area 51. It will live on your skin, your breath, your clothes, your hopes and wishes for days, weeks, months after. It will impregnate your molecules with an indelible funk. It will ruin your life, for you have duelled with the devil and lost, but finally, FINALLY, you can say you have truly lived. Cheddar is good too.

Scott and I shared a love of Époisses that bordered on the religious. Actually, maybe it was just me, but Scott seemed to be up for it anyway, and so off we went, a four-hour drive to Époisses for a trip that to me felt necessary, although, like everything at that point, the reasons why didn't seem entirely clear.

There are four *fromageries* – cheesemakers that make Époisses. The weird thing is that only one of them is actually in the town of Époisses. The rest are at least an hour from Époisses and, indeed, each other.

The first *fromagerie* we went to was the Fromagerie

159

Gaugry, an hour away from Époisses in some of the most expensive wine country in the world, the Côte de Nuit. They welcomed us in and let us have a walk around. We had turned up too late to see the cheese being made, but we did get a really wonderful, in-depth view of them cleaning down the surfaces. I mean, they were obsessive about cleaning their surfaces. They gave us a tasting of five cheeses, including Époisses and a glass of wine. It was 11 a.m. The cheese was extraordinary. It was a good start.

It went downhill from there. Next, we drove to Époisses itself. I was expecting Époisses to be full of artisanal cheese-makers, but the weird thing is, you get to Époisses and there's no mention of the cheese. It's a nothing sort of town. It's pretty, I suppose – it has an atmospheric old château in the middle of the town, surrounded by a forbidding moat, but there's nothing else save for the Fromagerie Berthaut. And you can't go into Fromagerie Berthaut like you can in the Fromagerie Gaugry, they just have a gift shop. We went to a local restaurant for lunch and they gave us a sliver of Époisses at the end of the meal and that was it.

'Something is going on here, Scott.' I said, as we finished up at the restaurant. 'I have two hypotheses: one – they're hiding something. There's something living in that Château d'Époisses – a gothic beast that lives on the blood of cheese virgins and shits out Époisses, or two: they're ashamed of the cheese they unleashed on the world and the damage it has done.'

'Yes. I'd imagine Hitler's home town doesn't have a big picture of him on the way in,' said Scott.

'We should ask the waiter,' I said.

'Don't do that,' said Scott.

We couldn't be bothered to try the last two fromageries.

That would have added another four hours of driving, so we got back into the car full of gently warming devil cheese and began our long journey home. We drove and drove and maybe it was the fumes from the Époisses but I felt like I had unusual clarity of thought. And then I started having the revelations.

'The thing is, they can't all be desperate to go. I mean, they're grown men. They could just hold it in,' I said as we trundled along the motorway. Scott and I were pondering one of the great French mysteries: why it is in France that you see so many men pissing by the side of the road.

The French love to piss in the open air. I remember once when he came round to our house quite early on in our friendship, Damien just started peeing in the garden. I was quite offended. I thought it was an attempt to show he was the alpha male, but I soon noticed that actually he does that everywhere. Whenever he gets the opportunity, he likes to pee in the open air. Albert, born in France, does it too. 'Just going for a wee!' he shouts as he pees in a rosemary bush at a wedding or funeral.

'Yes. There's more to it than that. Perhaps it's to do with the principles of liberty, equality and fraternity,' said Scott.

'Or perhaps it's just the thrill of a cool breeze against one's appendage. It's funny. It's normally the tradesmen doing the peeing, isn't it?' I mused. To me a cold wind against one's appendage didn't sound that appealing. Then, revelation no. 1.

'Holy crap. I think I've got it. They're scenting!' I exclaimed.

'What do you mean, they're scenting?' said Scott.

'That's why they're always peeing on the grass verges by the side of the road. They're communicating with each other. It has to be that!'

'Tommy, that's insane,' said Scott. I could tell by his voice that he actually thought it was plausible.

'They're letting each other know where they are, what jobs they are working on etc. If a plumber needs a length of nineteen-millimetre pipe, he might wee on a bush and another plumber will pass that bush, decipher his message and turn up with said pipe sometime after. That must be what's happening. What a relief. That had been bugging me ever since we got here.'

After a few moments of self-congratulation, I got on to thinking about how clean and ordered the fromagerie we visited was. It reminded me of Benoît's brewery. When you look around Benoît's brewery, what's most apparent is the organisation and the practical thinking that has gone into it. Suddenly, on that long straight motorway I had a realisation. *Benoît's brewery is just like Benoît. It's as if it's an extension of Benoît.* I thought about the other breweries I'd visited since I'd been in France. The Octopus Brewery on the outskirts of Orléans when I first got going, and the Petit Maiz Brewery in Tours, and when I thought about it, those breweries had the character of the brewer stamped all over them. They were extensions of the brewers. And then it came to me: revelation no. 2, and it was world-endingly awful. *If Benoît's Brewery is an extension of Benoît, then doesn't that mean that my brewery is an extension of me?* And at that moment I knew it to be true. It was undeniably true. It was desperate, was my brewery. It was sad and broken and ashamed of itself and there was no care to it. It felt like it had been given up on and most of all, its personal hygiene was appalling. It *was* me. Jill Dando the cat had been right all along.

These other breweries all had completely different

characters: some were more clinical, some had a more artisan feel, but they had things in common. They were logical, they had pride and honour and, most of all, they were clean. But when I looked around at my brewery, I saw insulation hanging from the ceiling, cobwebs, a floor that hadn't been cleaned in so long you could excavate Roman pottery from the layers of dried sludge. Bits of equipment everywhere. No order. No care taken. No love given to it. An acceptance that it was going down the pan, slowly disintegrating until it could no longer fulfil its purpose and it would be abandoned to the ivy already encroaching in the glassless windows.

'Ah crap.' I didn't have any pride in myself. It was true. It had gone. I can't tell you when – a long time ago, I think, but it had gone and if we were to turn this round, I needed to get it back.

Finally, revelation no. 3. I was pissed off with the whole thing. I got to thinking about my beers and I was so bored of them. The Biscuit Ale, the Cardinal IPA, the Clifton Porter. In truth, none of them were great even before all the problems I was having in the brewery. Diana had, for some time now, been going into my van and pulling out my labels and trailing them across the garden, much to Rose's displeasure. But I suspected she was trying to tell me some-thing. And then I had the revelation. She was telling me to forget about my old beers, the same four beers I'd been making for years now, and start expressing myself. Just like when she finally moved away from Charles and took up residence in Kensington Palace. She had to reinvent herself. She had to go out into the world and show everyone who she really was. Now I needed to start showing the world the real me. It was time to move to Kensington Palace.

What had stopped me making more than a very limited range of beers in the past was the cost of labels. I found that in order to get a good price on labels, I would have to order thousands and thousands of the same label and therefore make thousands and thousands of the same beer. Making the Christmas beers with their small quantities had forced me to look hard for a label printer who would do smaller print runs at a good price, and eventually I found one. They were a large multinational internet printing site and I hated using them because I liked using the local wine-label printers, but the truth was they were the only people that would print the small batches at a price I could afford. The customer service was terrible, they constantly made mistakes with the labels, they were always late, but they were cheap.

At the time I had the Christmas labels printed I hadn't really thought about what it meant to find a printer that would do short print runs, but now, thanks to Diana cleverly distributing my old labels across the garden, I realised the power that shorter print runs would give me. It meant I could make as many different beers as I wanted. I could do one-off beers, print 500 labels and move onto a different beer. And why not? That was the great advantage of being a small brewery like mine. I could be nimble.

I'd had this idea for a Saffron Pils for a while now. I think Tom Mathews the chef might have given it to me. Pilsner is a style of beer we might call lager. It originated in the town of Pilsen in the Czech Republic. I'd got the idea because we have several saffron growers in the Pays de Richelieu and I always like the idea of using local ingredients. I'd mentioned it to a couple of people and they'd said they didn't think it would work – if you got that earthy flavour, it wouldn't be great in a light beer – but it always made sense to me. It was a risk. Perhaps it was madness to do a beer like that when I really needed some decent beer to sell, but I had a feeling about it. I had to trust Diana.

I got home after the kids had gone to bed laden with the world's deadliest cheese, which had just benefited from four hours in a warm car, and a realisation that in order for the brewery to change, I would also have to change.

'Where have you been?' asked Rose.

'To Époisses,' I said.

'Oh right.' She wasn't even furious with me. More worryingly, she didn't even mention the smell. This was bad. 'You should probably check the news. They're locking down the country. Schools, shops and markets all shutting. The coronavirus is out of control. They've declared it a pandemic. I'm going to bed,' she said.

CHAPTER 11

It's surprisingly easy to avoid the mirror if you know there's something you don't want to see. You don't even do it consciously. It's an automatic thing and you can do it for months without ever seeing yourself. If you're brushing your teeth looking at the edge of the mirror, then I tell you now, something is wrong. Soon after the start of lockdown, Rose's family arranged a pub quiz via Zoom and the thing with Zoom is, you are right there on the screen. You can't avoid yourself and, holy crap, when we logged in and our image popped up on screen, Rose and me, suddenly there I was, looking absolutely awful. My face was red and puffed up. Bits of old Époisses stuck in my wildly out-of-control beard. Likewise my hair. I had a big bulbous nose. I looked like an alcoholic and that was not in the least surprising in retrospect, because I was drinking a lot. Since the beer had been going wrong I had really been drinking. It was lucky they couldn't smell me from the other side of the computer screen, because it wasn't great. Worst of all, I couldn't talk properly. *I couldn't actually talk properly.* I mumbled. I muddled up my words. I really looked at myself for the first time in months and in my face I could just see my decaying brewery, with shit everywhere.

You're never too old to go and get completely blasted. I'm not saying that. There's not much that beats getting really drunk every now and then, and it's good for you to get smashed once in a while. It cleanses the brain. It's like turning the computer off and on. But the problem is when you're drinking too much too regularly, because then being drunk isn't joyous any more. It's a morose experience. It's tiring. At best you're just getting back to where you should have been when you were sober. You're not getting the really fun drunken nights – you're getting nights sitting on the sofa in front of the TV that you can't see the point of, and the booze doesn't taste nice any more. And as you get older it's harder to recover, and when you have children who don't sleep and therefore you don't sleep, it magnifies everything by ten. All of a sudden, a couple of beers have you slurring. All of a sudden, you can feel your heart pounding in your chest when you lie down to sleep at night.

It wasn't like I was getting up in the morning and downing a bottle of cheap whisky. But I was drinking every evening now and sometimes it might have been one bottle of beer, but more often than not it was several. Or several glasses of wine.

I have always drunk a lot, especially in times of crisis. As I said before, that box of Fred's red, the most powerful wine ever to be produced, got me through a lot of stressful times. But this was different. This was spiralling. By the time lockdown happened and all the pressure had built to such a point, I'd been drinking heavily to try and cope, and then when I saw myself on that computer screen with Rose sitting next to me, I felt terrible. All my problems with the brewery and life in general were right there in front of me on a red puddle of a face. And, more than anything, I felt terrible for

Rose. To have to sit there with me looking like that in front of her family. To be associated with me. The shame of it.

Booze has really been an integral part of my life since I was in my teens. Booze has got me through tough times. When I was young, from my teens through into my late twenties, I was alone a lot. I had friends (don't make me list them), but I was alone, you know what I mean? And by the time I'd reached my thirties I'd resigned myself to being alone. I'd grown to like it and I'd grown to like drinking alone. I was looking forward to a gradual, solitary decline into a booze-soaked perishing. Then I met Rose and suddenly things changed, and then we had children and everything changed, but my attitude to drinking didn't. Not fundamentally. Now I was forced to confront it via Zoom and I had to change at least a little bit, and not for me. I had to change for my wife and family, for the sake of my brewery and, most importantly, for my poor blotchy nose.

There's not much to say about the lockdown that hasn't already been said because there was nothing else to do during the lockdown other than talk about the lock-down. In France we called it *le confinement* because we're better than you and we don't have a compulsion to name everything like a daytime game show hosted by a jaded ex-CBBC presenter whose only real credentials were that they'd survived #metoo. Apart from that, I don't think there was much difference between the experiences of the French and those of the British. They were firmer over here, I suppose. Rules were enforced rather than advised, but having spent four years in the French countryside, you realise they'd been preparing for this sort of thing for ever. You could drive around French villages for days without seeing anyone long before the lockdown. They voluntarily lived in lockdown most of the time already.

People pulled together. Because the markets were shut, the Boulangerie Subileau offered to stock my beer on their shelves and their kindness took me by surprise and I almost cried.

Monsieur Jean the bank manager phoned me up. I assumed he was going to shout at me for being overdrawn, but instead he ordered a load of beer for the staff at the bank. Now that is a bank manager. If they made a blueprint of the perfect bank manager, it would be Monsieur Jean.

I ran out of bottles and I couldn't afford to buy a whole pallet, so I phoned Benoît up and pretended there'd been a problem with the delivery of my bottles and I asked if he'd sell me a smaller quantity. He was happy to, of course. When I went round to get them and tried to pay Benoît with a cheque that would almost certainly have bounced, he winked and said, 'Don't worry, I'll send you an invoice. You can pay me then.' He knew. He bloody knew. To this day he's never sent me an invoice.

Oh, I tell you what, *le confinement* was singular for one absolutely masterful piece of French bureaucracy. I don't know this to be 100 per cent true, but I imagine in French government there is the Department for Paperwork, then there is the Department for Paperwork That You Should Have Signed First and finally there is the Department for Paperwork That You Needed To Sign After The Original Paperwork And Before The Paperwork That You Should Have Signed First. Somewhere in one of these offices, as the lockdown approached, a promising young paperwork inventor spotted an opportunity to show to the world that French bureaucracy was still unmatched.

It was announced during lockdown in France that you were only allowed out for certain reasons – shopping, exercise, compassionate grounds. If you wanted to go out, you had to sign a form to that effect. You could download the form from the government website. But the thing was, there was no one to approve it. You didn't have to send it off to the police for them to agree it. You only had to get yourself to sign it and then it was approved. You had to give yourself approval to go out. You actually had to print out a form, fill it out and then think to yourself – *Do I approve this person's request?* and if you did approve it, you signed it and you allowed yourself to do what you were going to do. It was an absolute masterpiece. I don't think it will ever be equalled. The time people wasted trying to get their printers to work. The paper, the printer ink. All so you could print out a form and sign it to tell yourself that you could go out. When everyone stood outside of an evening applauding the health workers who were saving lives, I too applauded those health workers, but a little bit of me was also applauding that man or woman who came up with the self-approved declaration. Bravo, young paperwork inventor, the future is yours.

'IIIIIIIIIIEEEEEEIIIIIIII will always love youuuuuuuuuuuooooouuu, IIIIEEEIII will always love youuuuuuuuuuuuuuuuuu.'

I didn't quite hit the last note, but there was no one else in the Richelieu Forest to hear me, so it didn't matter. Diana rustled out from the undergrowth and waddled to me. Paul Burrell had mentioned that 'I Will Always Love You' was Princess Diana's favourite song. Burt would never have come back on demand once he was in the forest, but

Diana would, as long as I sang. It was Diana, see? I knew it was. The night before, I had shaved my tatty beard off. Some people grow beards for the purposes of fashion but mine was solely a symbol of my laziness. I'd begun showering again and now I was running as fast as I could in the woods. For me it was part of my attempt to get myself into some kind of shape. I wanted to not despise myself again. And for Diana, well, I would never tell her this, but Diana, Princess of Wales was looking decidedly portly with all the special treats I had been giving her.

I was starting to realise why Diana was here. In her life, Diana had had to rebuild herself too. She was a woman who had spent much of her life crippled with self-doubt and self-esteem issues. In her final years with Prince Charles she was a shell of herself, but she had found a way to come back. She had emerged the other side with a confidence and a belief in her own place in the world. She had become the People's Princess; I needed to become the People's Brewer, and she was going to guide me.

We got back from the forest and I got into my World's Strongest Man training. I'd started training to be the World's Strongest Man, you see. I may not have mentioned that. I don't know if all strong men train like this, but I focused on press-ups, croissants, waddling around with kegs of beer and roaring like a mythical bear. But the best thing I did was go into the woods and just run as fast as I could. As we move into middle age, most of us don't really get the chance to just run flat out any more. When you're a kid in a playground you do it every day without thinking, but you stop doing it, like you stop doing lots of fun things as you get older. When was the last time you did it? Just run as fast as you possibly can? I'm telling you, it feels brilliant.

I'd hurtle down these little forest tracks, arms flailing, occasional blood-curdling screams, rabbits and deer diving left and right into the scrub in absolute terror, and it felt like I was running so fast my feet were barely touching the ground. So fast that the world blurred as it rushed past me, as if I was entering warp speed. Of course, to a passer-by it would have looked like a fat man barely exiting a jog, but it felt fast to me. I didn't tell anyone I was training to be the World's Strongest Man, save for my dog, who had been possessed by Princess Diana. They might think I was mad. It felt good to lift kegs and waddle around and roar and run as fast as I could – like I was letting something out.

'Are you OK, Tommy? I heard some roaring,' said Rose.

I emerged from behind the van on our driveway.

'Yep fine, just moving some kegs.' I was fine. Training for World's Strongest Man had been going well. I wasn't noticeably any stronger, but I had already perfected several roars – Bear Startled in the Night, Disappointed Lion, and only today Jilted Leopard. I was still trying for my greatest roar though, a roar I would call Moon Tiger. I followed Rose back into the kitchen.

'Hey Rose, what do you think of this?' I said, showing her a picture on my phone. We drank cappuccinos round the kitchen table.

'We don't need a four-poster bed, Tommy. We've already got a four-poster bed,' said Rose, handing it back to me.

'No, for Diana. I don't think we can have her sleeping on that old rug any more.'

'What? No!' Rose looked at Burt/Diana sprawled out on his rug – a hairy fire extinguisher with legs. 'He looks pretty happy to me.'

In truth, we didn't have the €600 to ship the four-poster

dog's bed from China, so I was quite pleased Rose said no, but it was important for me that Diana knew I was looking out for her.

I began tackling the brewery and I began tackling myself, because since the brewery was essentially me, it now made sense that for everything that needed changing in the brewery, there must be some root cause coming from my life that I also had to change. With Diana at my side, I undertook a forensic examination that lasted several weeks, and finally we got to the bottom of what was going wrong and it was really quite simple: as Benoît had suspected, I wasn't cleaning the heat exchanger adequately, so that the beer was vulnerable to bacterial infections. Oh, also, there was much too much oxygen getting to the beer during the bottling process. And the joints on the fermenters weren't clean and often they weren't airtight, which meant both the possibility of bacterial infection and oxidation. Also, when I cold crashed, I hadn't noticed that the beer shrank as it got colder, sucking the liquid in the airlock at the top of the fermenter into it, making it susceptible to infections again. Oh, and the thermometer in the fermenter was located towards the bottom, just below where I'd wrapped insulation around to make the cooling of the fermenter more efficient. This meant that the thermometer reading was actually several degrees warmer than the majority of the beer, which was wrapped in insulation, so I'd been unknowingly cold crashing my beer in the minuses, which does all sorts of things to the flavours and the oxygen intake. Plus, a while ago I'd started using a new bittering hop – Brewers Gold – because I liked the name, but it turned out Brewers Gold is a riddle of a hop. It's not that bitter in terms of alpha and beta acids, but it has a really strong flavour

173

around the bitterness. It lasts on your palate like a well-hit gong. It's tempting to think of bittering hops as giving little else other than bitterness – certainly the aromatic oils and stuff that hops contain get blown away the longer they're left in the boil – but there are other flavours that remain and, depending on the hop, they can be really strong. Brewers Gold doesn't have great bitterness, but it still needs to be used delicately, otherwise it can give the beer a sour flavour. Plus, I had been experimenting with spices and speciality malts that I really had no idea how to use. Also, there was a seal on the faucet of one of the plastic fermenters that hadn't been installed properly and it meant a load of old gunk had gathered in a crack there and whenever I moved my beer from the fermenter to the bottling tank, all the beer passed over this gunky seal, making it susceptible to contamination. And I wasn't leaving my beers to clear for long enough. Also, the brewery in general was unsanitary. The floor. The ceiling. Cobwebs falling into the beer. The air itself. The muddied hoses that the beer passed through. And finally, Burt. Don't ask me how, but Burt. I know Burt had gone and been replaced by Princess Diana, but still, Burt. The ghost of Burt.

Diana was by my side in the garden while I ground my malt. We were preparing to brew in the coming days, so I was working through our checklist to make sure we'd done everything we could.

'So, we've now pumped water through the plate chiller at high pressure and cleaned and sanitised it. The question, Diana, is how it relates to me. What do I need to do to clean my "spiritual plate chiller", if you like?'

'Colonic irrigation,' said Diana, without prompting. I should say Diana didn't actually speak to me. I wasn't at the point where I was hearing voices, but sometimes I could imagine Diana and Jill Dando the cat speaking to me, and that's different, I think.

'Yes. I'm not really up for that, Diana. I was thinking maybe I should try and floss more. OK, to try and stop oxygen contamination, we've got new clamps on all the hoses. We're now passing CO_2 through the pump before we transfer the wort to the bottling tank. That's about as good as we're going to get. What does this mean for me? How can I stop the leaks around my "spiritual bottling plant"? Maybe I'm being influenced by outside forces to my detriment. I feel like it's a mental thing, you know? Like I'm not clarifying my thoughts.'

'Colonic irrigation,' said Diana. Princess Diana was an outspoken fan of colonic irrigation.

'I'll try some kind of meditation. OK, after that, we've done our best to improve the general sanitation of the brewery. We've hoovered all the cobwebs. Cleaned the floor as best we can. Cleaned all the joints. But how do I clean my "spiritual fermenter joints"?'

'That's definitely colonic irrigation,' said Diana.

'I'll shower more. Now this is interesting. Ever since we started using Brewers Gold, our blonde beer has had a funny flavour,' I continued. 'We are now aware of the capricious nature of the Brewers Gold. We will modify our quantities. But the question is, how does this—'

'Colonic irrigation,' said Diana.

'Right. Now, finally, a lot of our problems started coming about when we were cold crashing the beer. To combat this, we've adjusted the insulation so that it covers the whole fermenter now, and at the start of the cold crash we are taking out some of the liquid from the airlock so it doesn't get sucked in. But what is my spiritual cold crash? Don't say colonic irrigation.'

Diana thought for a moment. 'You need to stick a hosepipe up your arse and fill your bowels with water,' she said.

Two rabbits arrived. We kept them in the rabbit hutch in the garden. I presumed they were part of Rose's pregnancy cravings, which was odd because she hadn't been pregnant for nearly two years.

Brew day: Richard Pils

Malts
- Heisenberger Pilsner
- Carapils
- Biscuit

Hops
- Brewers Gold
- Magnum
- Sajvinjski Goldings
- Triskel

Other additions
- Saffron at the end of the boil

Yeast
- AEB lager yeast

Saffron is a funny ingredient. It's got earthiness; it's got a warmth; it's also perfumed, floral, luxurious. You know it's something exceptional, but at the same time it's a virtuoso; it's Princess Diana; it's a flamboyant yet lonely ingredient, and more often than not it doesn't fit in and tragedy follows. Adding saffron to a recipe can be like signing an ageing Brazilian maestro to play for Leyton Orient – it might be wonderful, he might take them to heights they haven't seen since 1961, but more likely than not he'll spend his nights in Essex nightclubs, he won't track back, and they'll get relegated.

A proper Czech pilsner is made exclusively with a hop called Saaz, one of the 'noble hops'. It's a beautiful hop, is Saaz. It's worshipped. It's unmistakable. It's really expensive too, so I didn't use it. Besides, I didn't want too much hop in it. I wanted the saffron to come through, but then not too much, because equally I didn't want too much saffron in it. A beer that truly tastes of saffron wouldn't be good. Beer should taste of beer. It needed to add something to the beer without making it taste of saffron, like the Belgians would do it. I bought some local saffron from Agnès, a saffron grower I knew from the local producers' shop in Chaveignes. I had a clear vision of what I wanted. A light pilsner, 4.5–5 per cent volume alcohol, a beer to drink in the sun but something with a bit of character. Something to differentiate it from the omnipresent Kronenbourg, and I felt like the saffron would do that. Until recently I hadn't been able to make pilsners because the yeast you use to ferment pilsners works at 12 to 14° C and I couldn't control my fermenter temperatures to that degree, but now I had my chiller unit I could maintain a low temperature in the fermenter.

I milled my grain the night before – mostly pilsner malt, a little bit of Carapils and some biscuit malt, because I think biscuit malt gives a beer a sort of full stop when you drink it.

177

The morning of the brew I said some positive affirmations with Princess Diana. I got in early, around 8 a.m., and set everything up. That godforsaken brewery. It was still grim in there.

I ran an extra sanitising cycle through the heat exchanger and I mashed in the grains. I was looking at a low mash temperature – 63° C – because I wanted a nice dry lager.

The brew went smoothly until the boil, when I heard frantic barking outside.

Diana was sitting in my van minding her own business. I could still hear the barking. It was Louis, hovering by the hedge behind the rabbits' cage. He'd managed to push the fencing to the point where he'd created a gap large enough for the rabbits to escape, which they had duly done and now he was hunting for them in the bushes.

'Oh, for Christ's sake, Louis,' I said. Then I remembered my brew. I got back to the brewery, chucked in all the saffron I could afford with eight minutes left of the boil, because I didn't want it to be in there too long and have a lot of its flavour boiled off. I racked the beer off into the fermenter, pitched the yeast and went to see if I could find the rabbits. I couldn't. Louis had chased them out of the garden, never to be seen again.

'*Et tu*, Louis?' I said, and I felt pleased with myself for a moment. And then I realised I'd have to tell Albert that the rabbits escaped.

And that is how you brew saffron pils.

Pilsners take longer to ferment out. It was over a month till I could try it. So I focused on other things. I still had malt. I still had hops. I could still brew. Another new beer. It was time to get wild. A tonka milk stout.

178

Brew day: Tonka Milk Stout

Malts
- Pale malt
- Rolled barley
- Crystal (medium)
- Chocolate malt
- Patent malt
- Roasted barley

Hops
- East Kent Goldings

Other additions
- Lactose
- Ground tonka beans in fermenter

Yeast
- American West Coast

Milk stouts are stouts made with lactose – the sugar you find in milk. Normal brewer's yeast ferments out most of the sugar in beer, but it doesn't ferment lactose, so the lactose stays in the beer, giving it a sweetness and a thick, creamy mouthfeel. It's hard to describe the flavour of the tonka bean, but roughly it's in between vanilla and almond. You need to taste it. A tonka-bean stout isn't an original idea – lots of people have done it before me – but it appealed to me because French dark beers – *brunes* – tend to be sweet. People would be taken aback when they tried my Clifton Porter to find it wasn't sweet at all. I thought a tonka milk stout might appeal to people who liked French *brune*.

With stouts you often get an acrid taste, which is actually quite desirable, but I wanted this to be a smoother, sweeter stout, so the day before I cold steeped the dark grains. To get the colour and flavour of a stout, you use a small percentage of grains that have been kilned longer and therefore are darker. It's only around 10 per cent of the grain bill you use – the rest might be similar to a pale ale – but that 10 per cent of dark grains makes a huge difference. I used to add 15 or even 20 per cent, but I've learned over time that the less you use, the better. I go as low as 6 or 7 per cent now. It turns the colour of the beer black and gives torrified flavours – coffee, chocolate, ashtray. However, if you cold steep the dark grains – the roasted barley, the patent malt and the chocolate malt – that is to say, leave them in cold water overnight and then add the wort (now black) to the copper after the mash, you really mute some of the acrid flavour. Aside from pale malt, patent malt, roasted barley and chocolate malt, I added a decent amount of rolled barley to really thicken the beer. I mashed at 63° C. My thoughts were that with the lactose and the rolled barley, I didn't need to worry about trying to get any extra richness from the mash. I wasn't sure how much lactose to use – I could have googled it, but instead I just guessed and chucked in three kilograms for a 200-litre batch. I like to chance my arm. I got it in the fermenter and pitched the yeast – a West Coast American strain, a neutral, forgiving yeast – at 19° C.

And that is how you brew Tonka Milk Stout.

There was one fermenter left. I decided I would try and brew the Berger Blonde again, because I felt like I owed it to Damien to brew a decent Berger Blonde. It was his name on the label. But first I had to do something.

'*Coucou* Tommy, *coucou* Albert!' said Colleen as we

walked past the paddocks, along the driveway to their house at the edge of the forest.

'*Salut,* Tommy! We haven't seen you in ages,' called Celia. They were both in the field tending to the horses.

'*Salut!*' I called back, a pack of beers in one hand, pétanque balls in the other. Albert waved and hid behind my legs. Zoë ran out and had about three conversations with us in French before I could offer a word. Then she and Albert charged off to push each other over on the trampoline.

I found Damien and, even though I hadn't really spoken to him in months, we didn't exchange pleasantries. We went to the dirt track at the back of their house that leads to the forest. I handed him the beers. He popped the caps off two of them with the end of a cigarette lighter, handed one back to me and we began to play pétanque. It was as if I'd only seen him the night before.

You might know pétanque as boules. You've almost certainly played it if you've been on holiday to France. You take a little wooden ball we call the jack and the French call the *cochonnet*, which I think must mean piglet or something, because *cochon* is pig, and you throw it a few metres away. Then you throw larger metal balls at it. It's a simple game.

We don't really say much when we play pétanque. You don't need to say much. Talking ruins it. You throw the balls, drink beer and forget about everything else. The music is the clack of the balls as they fall on each other and dive in different directions. It's the French equivalent of meditation.

Damien always won. He'd normally let me get a few points. It didn't matter. It's a nice way to pass the time and that's all we really want, isn't it.

I had an ulterior motive for playing pétanque with

Damien. I had developed a theory about the blonde beer. We'd been seeing much less of Damien and Celia as the year went on. We were very busy, but you know – you can still meet up if you put the effort in, can't you? I don't know what it was really, but we were drifting away from them. That's what it felt like to me.

I'd realised that the Berger Blonde beer had started to go wrong long ago at pretty much the same time that we'd started seeing less and less of the Bergers. And even when the other beers were starting to get better, the blonde still came out badly. It occurred to me that there might be a correlation.

I don't believe in spirituality because honestly, what does that mean? No, I believe in science, evidence, facts, bricks, mortar, calculators, robots, hiding one's emotions, the sound of car doors shutting, World's Strongest Man on Channel 5 – that's me – but recently things were shifting. I mean there was the *pain tradition* at Subileau's bakery – that couldn't be explained, unless you were willing to entertain the notion of magic elves, and then Burt had been possessed by Princess Diana, and now I didn't know anything any more, you know? I was floating in space. I was starting to feel like there was something else out there, and the more I thought about it, the more I thought I knew why the Berger Blonde wasn't coming out right. It seemed to me that the state of the Berger Blonde was a reflection of our relationship with the Bergers. The more we drifted from the Bergers, the more the beer came out sour. So, if I could rekindle the relationship – a game of pétanque, you see – then maybe the beer would come back as well?

I brewed the blonde the next day and waited.

You can argue that if you have enough monkeys at type-writers they'll write the complete works of Shakespeare, and if you give them enough booze they'll write *A Beer in the Loire* or whatever, but however you want to look at it, whether it was a moment of genius or total fluke, the moment I tried my new Saffron Pils, I knew I'd struck gold.

It wasn't the finished article. It was a little too bitter and although the saffron was there, it needed more of it. I wanted it to be luxurious. It needed a richer mouthfeel, but I knew I had the makings of something. Most importantly, it was clean.

The tonka stout came out well too. That was also a little too bitter – bitterness takes away from the smoothness – but it was a good beer. It was clean.

Before I tried the Berger Blonde, I invited Damien and Celia over for a barbecue, just to make sure I'd done what I could for our relationship.

Bavette is a cut of beef we call flank. I don't think we use it much in the UK. Whenever I have the chance, I barbecue it. You can get it in thick, foot-long strips. You rub it in oil, chuck loads of salt on it and cook it really hot for a little time on both sides and leave the inside bloody. But the best bit is the sauce.

Have you ever been to the Relais de Venise? Sometimes it's known as Entrecôte. It started as a restaurant in Paris and now it has branches all over the place. I went to one down on Marylebone Lane in London a couple of times. There's no menu and the only thing they ask you is how you want your steak done (answer – blue). You get a salad to start, with a bit of bread. Do NOT ask for butter. You're not allowed it. You'll get told off like my Aunt Myra did once. Then they bring you the most fantastic chips and sliced steak, but it's the sauce that makes it. Their legendary green secret sauce.

I decided to cook *bavette* on the barbecue for Damien and Celia and try to recreate the Relais de Venise's secret sauce. Unbeknown to our guests, the sauce wasn't going to plan.

'Try this,' I said to Damien.

I thrust a bottle of the new Berger Blonde at him. Damien poured it slowly, careful to leave the deposit in the bottle. He knew my beers well. All beers that are bottle conditioned have a little deposit in them, because you are re-fermenting the beer in the bottle, which means that once the sugar has been eaten up, the dead yeast cells drop to the bottom of the beer. At Braslou Bière we have a little bit more deposit than most. In fact, in some of my beers it's not just dead yeast in the bottle, it's hop particles, it's spiders legs, it's old bank cards, Viking relics; the deposit is deep.

'It's good. It's much better!' said Damien.

I knew it was better as well. I'd already tried it. The beer had been healed. I wanted to explain that it was because we had been playing pétanque and the beer was dependent on the strength of our relationship. I wanted to explain that Princess Diana had possessed Burt, that Jill Dando was the cat, that there were magic pixies in the Subileau bakery. I wanted to explain that the brewery was me and I was the brewery and I had improved my personal hygiene.

'The second child is easier than the first,' I said, and left it at that.

The *bavette* was ready. I went inside to get the sauce.

There are several recipes online that claim to be the secret sauce of the Relais de Venise, but I didn't bother to look at any of them. I'd made it a couple of times before and

I thought I remembered how to do it. I cooked and blitzed the chicken livers with some mustard, cream, shallots and parsley. When it was finished it didn't look like I remembered it looking.

'Oh my God, Tommy. What is that?' exclaimed Celia. There was terror in her voice. I put the bowl of sauce on the table and people backed up. It was supposed to be green. Instead it was pink. There was too much chicken liver in it and not nearly enough parsley. Also, and this is a real no-no when it comes to making sauces, my sauce wasn't a sauce. It was thick and wobbly. I hadn't added enough water. I'll tell you what it looked like, and I apologise for this, but it looked like someone had had their brains blown out of the back of their head and it had landed in the bowl in the middle of the table. I offered it round the table as people either politely declined or fainted. Colleen heroically took a teaspoonful.

'At least it tastes nice,' said Colleen.

'Thanks, Colleen,' I said. I will always remember Colleen for that.

I put some on my meat and I looked at it there – pink, gelatinous, wobbling on top of the rare beef – and I almost threw up. But I had to prove it was OK because of some deep-seated insecurities that I haven't dared to face, and so I ate it – and I think I am still eating it today when I shut my eyes.

The point was, the Berger Blonde was fine. In fact, it was better than fine. It was the best Berger Blonde I'd made. I had three good beers. I couldn't remember the last time I'd had three good beers.

I thought of new beer recipes. We all assumed *le confinement* would be over in a month or so. The Fête de l'Asperge – the asparagus festival at Braslou – would be coming around in May. I had an idea for an asparagus beer – why not? A wheat beer with Polaris hops and local asparagus in the boil. The first of its kind in all the world. I was bored of my Cardinal IPA. The premise behind it was using European hops to make an American-style IPA, and it was an interesting beer in that respect, but the cold, hard truth was those hops I was using – Callista, Ariana – weren't as pleasant in that style of beer as the American hops. They contained some of the characteristics I desired – they had some citrus-fruit flavours to them, but they also had spicy and grassy flavours, and you just don't want them in a light IPA like that. So I came up with two new IPAs – a red IPA called Sang de Braslou (Blood of Braslou) and a blonde IPA made with lots of wheat called Lait de Braslou (Milk of Braslou). The red IPA would be more like an old-style American West Coast IPA with a good amount of bitterness and some crystal malt, and the blonde IPA would be more in the style of an East Coast IPA – less bitter, tropical in flavour. We still didn't have any money really, but there was the chance of a future. Around the house it was jollier. I was jollier. I could breathe again. Once the sun came out and we got to the Fête de l'Asperge, nothing could stop us!

The sun shone through most of *le confinement*. I built the children a go-cart track out of pallets and these big metre-wide plastic boards that act as shelves when you order a pallet of bottles, which kept them entertained/fighting each other for at least a month.

A miniature goat arrived. I presumed it must have been part of Rose's pregnancy cravings and so on. We got the goat, Olaf, from Monsieur Richard's son, Denis. Olaf was a peaceful goat. A sort of middle-management type who'd been happily working the same job for years and going home to do jigsaw puzzles. We'd heard about goats being excellent escape artists, but Denis reckoned we wouldn't need any extra fencing because Olaf was pretty tranquil, and he was right. Olaf was content to wander around the orchard at the back, chewing at leaves.

Le confinement caused beer sales to plummet. That's a lie – there wasn't a long way for them to fall. But they hit the very bottom just as they should have been picking up.

Meanwhile, I brewed when I could. By May the kids were going nuts. There was no sign of lockdown ending. The Marché de l'Asperge had been cancelled, which was an enormous blow. It's so hard to get any work done with young children around all the time. They demand your attention; they are masters at emotional blackmail; Margot took to sneaking into the brewery and mixing all the bottles up in the boxes, so I never knew what beer I had left, but we were in no position to complain. We had space for the kids to run around. We had a forest over the road. I thought of my old neighbours back in London, who lived in the flat next door to me with their two children and no outdoor space whatsoever. Not even a balcony. I've no idea how families like that got through it.

I could still brew a bit. And I knew that even if I couldn't sell it now, by the time lockdown ended, I would have stock to get me well into summer and if I had a good summer and sold all my stock, then by the end of the year I'd pretty much be where I would have been anyway.

I tried to cut down my drinking, you know? It wasn't that successful, in all honesty. The *confinement* was unsettling. I remember when they declared it, the first thing we did was go and buy a bottle of whisky. I'm glad we did. The first night of *confinement* I locked all the gates and put the shutters up on the house. I'm not sure what I was expecting – faceless hordes to emerge from the forest or something. I wasn't sure what, but it was unsettling.

I was becoming more and more troubled by the thought that the brewery was an extension of me, and the more I contemplated it, the more depressed I got. Because when you extrapolate it, it's not just the brewery that's an extension of you, is it? It's everything. Everything you touch is an extension of you. Your bedroom, your car. The way you treat things. The way you treat people. That's *you*. It sounds obvious when you write it down – of course that's you, but for me it wasn't obvious. I was always waiting for the true me to come to the fore. 'Oh, once we've got the brewery going properly, I'll get it all tidied up. I'll fix up the crumbling walls. I'll install a proper ceiling. Everything will be ordered. I've just got to wait for the sales to start rising – for the kids to get back to school. Once everything is in place, I'll sort the brewery out.' But I wasn't going to sort it out. There'd be something else and then something else. Since I was a teenager, I'd been waiting for everything to fall into place. But of course there wasn't a true version of me around that corner. *This* was me. And I was like that with everything, not just the brewery. The perfect example was the bar that Damien had made out of pallets that he'd given me after his wedding. It was a great little bar: it had chalkboards to mark up which beer was on which pump; it had cup holders on the sides; it had pieces of driftwood that had been varnished as the shelves. I used it once and then I left it in the garden. It rained. I left it. It got hot and I left it. All I had to do was put it away, but I couldn't. It wasn't even laziness. On some level it was a deliberate act. I told myself

I'd get around to putting it away once I'd done other things. It would have taken ten minutes, but I didn't do it and in the end it sat in the garden for weeks and it got warped and it started to deteriorate and was almost useless. I watched this happen and I couldn't seem to do anything about it. It was self-destructive behaviour – it didn't make any sense. Something in me was broken. Deep down I didn't believe I deserved any success. That was what it was, and that had been there for as long as I could remember and it manifested itself in an all-permeating, absurdist desire to fail. When I looked back, it had always been there at the edge of all of my humiliations, watching on, this overwhelming desire to screw everything up.

It didn't feel like I could get rid of it – it was too dug in, but I started to think that now I had outed it, maybe I could combat it if I was determined. So that is what I began to do. I had to recognise when I was deliberately messing things up and then, if I really tried, I could change my behaviour. So I tried to cut down on the drinking a bit, but it was really hard. It felt like it might all be too late. We were effectively broke. The beer I was brewing was good, that was what was so frustrating – but the bars had shut, the restaurants had shut, the markets had shut.

Brew day: Sang de Braslou IPA

Malts
- Red X
- Cara Munich
- Crystal (medium)

Hops

- Columbus
- Cascade (from Alsace)
- Hallertau Callista
- Mandarina Bavaria

Other adjuncts

- Hibiscus in the boil (for colour)

The night before, another miniature goat had arrived. Albert named him Twinkle. We got him because we thought Olaf was lonely. Twinkle was younger than Olaf. I had a feeling about Twinkle.

For my new IPA, Sang de Braslou, I used Red X malt because I was aiming for a blood-coloured beer, but I still wanted the hops to be the most prominent. You can use Red X as a base malt, you see, and I think it's not as malty as something like Munich malt. I used to love Sierra Nevada Pale Ale. When that first came out in the pubs in London, it blew my tiny mind. So I wanted to make something along those lines.

I mashed in as normal and then, as normal, I got a call from the mayor to tell me one of our animals had escaped.

'Hi, Tommy, *ça va?*' said Madame Leclerc, the Mayor of Braslou.

'Yes, fine. How are you?'

'All fine here. One thing – one of your goats is down here at the *mairie.*'

'Aha. How did you know it was one of ours? Actually, don't answer that. I'm on my way.' I knew it would be Twinkle that had escaped. Olaf wasn't into that sort of thing. And sure enough, Olaf was happily pottering around the orchard while Twinkle was nowhere to be seen.

I had an hour to get to the *mairie* and catch Twinkle before I needed to mash out. This called for the help of a three-year-old.

'Albert! We need to catch Twinkle.'

'OK Daddy. Erm, you're a spotty bottom.'

'Exactly. Let's go.' We jumped into the car and headed for central Braslou – a three-minute drive.

By the time we were at the *mairie*, Twinkle the goat had moved on. After several unconfirmed sightings, we got a call to say someone had found him in their garden just around the corner. By now we had formed a posse. There was me, Albert, Madame Leclerc and the secretary from the *mairie*.

Twinkle was happily chewing the shrubs in some poor elderly woman's garden. The four off us fanned out to try and get close enough to Twinkle to catch him, but whereas three of us adopted a stealth approach, one of us – I won't say who, because he's only three and I don't want to harm his chances of future employment – opted for a sort of Viking berserker approach. Every time we got close to the goat, this one member of our party would charge at it, shouting at the top of his voice. One thing that is crucial to catching a goat is an integrated approach. This wasn't working.

As word spread that there was a goat on the loose in downtown Braslou, more and more people came to see what was going on. Grandmas came down with their granddaughters to watch. Soon we had fifteen men (well, me), women and toddlers all chasing a miniature goat round a garden. After half an hour of goat chasing as the elderly women of Braslou roared us on, we managed to push Twinkle into a garage area, more by luck than planning.

'Stand back, everyone. This is between me and the goat,' I said. The crowd, absolutely stunned by my bravery, duly stood back and watched as I followed Twinkle into the garage.

Apart from a stab of light from a straining sun across the back wall, it was shadows of lawnmowers, watering cans, chainsaws. Echoes of bats hung in the air, reminding me that I had left my kingdom; now I was an intruder in a world of death and massacre and blood and destruction and garden storage. Total silence reigned, save for the scurry of a rat or the rustle of a giant spider. Shadows of plant pots, lined high up on shelves, seemed to expand and morph into sinister dancing top hats. I began my search: meticulous, brave, incredibly brave. I moved gardening equipment from one horrifying dark corner to the next. Twinkle was in here somewhere. He was waiting for me.

Cut a long story short, I found him in the corner. Well, he found me. I got to the back of the garage and Twinkle, in a bid to outflank me, leapt up against a wall and literally bounced into my arms. I emerged a hero, clutching that goat as I staggered into the daylight, and the whole of Braslou cheered. That's what it felt like. But then, as the local women brought their children in to stroke the cute little goat, Twinkle let out an ugly, human-sounding scream and it completely ruined the moment. Everyone went home disappointed. I got back to the brewery with moments to spare and started sparging my grains.

The big difference with an IPA like that and a normal beer is the sheer amount of hops one uses, and when one adds those hops. With a normal beer, the hops will all be added while the wort is boiling. This is good practice, as it sterilises the hops, so anything that might be on them that could ruin the beer is killed, but the problem is, for every moment you boil hops, or indeed leave hops in water above 80° C they are losing the aromatic hop oils that constitute a large part of their flavour. So with this beer, because I wanted some genuine bitterness, I added my bittering hops, Columbus, at the start of the boil, but for my aroma hops I finished the boil and then cooled my beer down to around 70° C before adding my flavouring hops – Cascade (a classic American IPA hop) and Hallertau Callista. I wasn't sure about using Callista any more – it didn't really work out in a New England-style IPA because it was a bit too spicy, but with the stronger flavours of a bitter, malty IPA like this, I thought it might have a chance, and I had loads of it left over, so I had to do something with it. Finally, a bit of Mandarina Bavaria, which gives a particular orange flavour. Once the hops were in, I stirred the beer for thirty minutes and then moved it to the fermenter.

I should say, I added the hibiscus at the end of the boil. The hibiscus was mostly for colour – to give the beer a real red colouring. You have to be careful with hibiscus though, because it's tart. It can add to the bitterness of the beer.

Twinkle was hurled back into his orchard with Olaf to tell of his adventures and I took a tour of the fencing to try and work out how he escaped.

And that is how you brew Sang de Braslou IPA.

'*Salut*, Damien.' I called over the gate. During *le confinement* we weren't even supposed to mix with our neighbours.

'*Salut*. How's it going?'

'Yeah, not bad. How are you?'

'Yeah, really good. I've given up booze. Haven't had a drop for three weeks.'

'Oh, for Christ's sake, Damien,' I whispered under my breath.

In most places during *le confinement*, people reported much less pollution and the return of nature. Birds returned, as did forest animals that would normally have been scared by all the human activity that was now on hold. In the Pays de Richelieu not so much. You see, during the lockdown, I started a home-delivery service. Throughout March and April, the tranquillity of the countryside was torn to shreds by the sound of the Tub of Thunder (don't make me say it) zig-zagging across the countryside, siren blaring, lights flashing, black smoke pumping from the exhaust, metal grinding other metal as rabbits dived down their rabbit holes and deer retreated to the furthest depths of the forest. It was comforting to see that despite the global pandemic the roads were still lined with French tradesmen peeing in the bushes. I knew now that they were just checking on each other, making sure they were OK.

'Pierre, I hear your wife left you. If you need someone to talk to, just piss in this lay-by,' they were probably saying.

I enjoyed the deliveries. I would sign my form each day to give myself approval to do it; sometimes I'd interrogate myself to check I was who I said I was. A delivery service was a valid reason to get out of the house and it felt like I was actually doing something, but it wasn't enough. I was barely breaking even once I took in the cost of petrol. Months and months of disastrous sales were finally taking their toll. I owed everyone money. Just before we became destitute, the French government stepped in. Because of the Covid-19 pandemic they offered financial aid to businesses like mine. They worked out what you had made that quarter of the year compared to the same time last year, and if you weren't making the same money, they would give you €1,500 a month. Compared to the year before I was doing terribly. I was nowhere near what I'd earned the previous year. It had nothing to do with the virus, of course – it was because for six months I hadn't been able to make a decent beer, but the reason didn't matter. We were eligible for the solidarity funds. It wasn't a huge amount, but it could just about keep us going through the lockdown. In fact, while I'm not going to make light of the crisis – it's a global catastrophe and I live in fear of my parents getting the virus – in a weird, selfish way it saved us. Without the lockdown we'd have been adrift with no money whatso-ever. Suddenly, because of the virus the government were giving us enough money to live for a few months and we had a reprieve. And now that I'd solved the problems in the brewery, because I was using my new equipment correctly – the chiller unit and the double-walled fermenter – the beer was coming out better than it had ever done before. It was a reset button, the lockdown. It helped us in some ways. Everything stopped. It was like the safety car coming out at the Indy 500: it didn't matter how well or badly you'd been doing, suddenly we were all bunched up together again and ready to restart.

'The thing is, Fred, I owe them more than I'm getting from the government in an entire month. There's no way I can pay them. Also, I've noticed my toenails are going a bit yellow. Is that a fungal infection, do you think?' I said.

Fred looked thoughtful. Then he got a bottle of fizz out of his fridge.

First they send you a couple of reminders, you see. It

doesn't seem that serious. Then they send you a recorded letter. That's embarrassing because the postie has to deliver it to you by hand and round here you know the postie and the postie knows everyone and the postie knows exactly what the letter is. Then, if you still don't pay, you get the call. That's when you're in trouble. Because once they start phoning you, if you can't pay, then presumably, sooner or later, the bailiffs come.

I was three months late with my payment to the bottle company. I was late paying other companies too, but the bottling company were the first to get heavy. I knew the others would follow. I'd had the two reminders. Now the letter arrived recorded delivery. I owed them around €2,000. With the government handouts, that was all we got a month. There was nothing left of it once we'd bought food, paid the utilities bills and so on. I couldn't pay the bottle company. There were other bills as well. Taxes to pay. So many taxes. I wasn't even close to being able to afford to pay for the bottles. I phoned them and told them I'd pay the following week. Then the following week I emailed them and said I'd pay the week after. I was stalling for time.

How do bailiffs work? Do they take your most valuable goods? Most of our money was in the brewery equipment – were they going to take that? Because if they did, then that was it. What would the kids say when they arrived? What would Rose say?

I felt like Al Capone. After all the murders and other terrible crimes he committed, they got him on a tax-evasion charge. I'd always imagined that my downfall would come in the shape of the brewery burning down or that I'd poisoned half of the Richelais or something like that, yet here I was about to be undone by a bill for some empty bottles.

We sold what we could. The truth was, it wasn't really working out with Gadget. We'd had him a couple of years and he was grumpy sod. We got Bella the Cameroonian sheep in to cheer him up, and it worked in a way, because now he had someone to pick on. He'd charge her and bite bits of fur off her back if he caught her, and he seemed genuinely happy for a little while. But then as it went on, he just found her incredibly annoying, and the thing with sheep is they are not bright. Bella was hardwired to follow other animals – in this case Gadget – so she would wander around directly behind him, which really started to irritate him, and so he'd chase her off and whatever, but she would just carry on doing it because that was all she knew to do. Follow Gadget. It was an abusive relationship and eventually we had to do something about it. We put them both up for sale.

No one wanted to buy Gadget. He gave off grumpy vibes even in photograph form, but we had some interest in Bella. A lady from Tours agreed to buy her, so we arranged for her to come down and pick her up at the end of June. It was a sad time. Bella was the only animal who hadn't betrayed me.

Margot now ruled the house. She partied all night and in the day she sat at the end of the dining table in the kitchen, roaring at me like Henry VIII. She was a year and a half old.

'JUICE!' she'd shout. 'YOGGIE,' she'd demand.

'The second child is easier than the first,' I'd whisper to myself as I hid behind the sofa.

To best highlight what life is like before and after having children, we must consider going for a crap. Before children, one can pass an entire morning on the loo reading newspapers, practising mindfulness, reflecting on the week's events as one's legs go numb. It's a pleasant experience. However, going for a crap when you're in charge of young children goes more like this:

'POO MEDICINE! POO MEDICINE! POO MEDICINE!' A three-year-old shouts at you as you cower on the loo, and they spray you repeatedly in the eyes with Beyoncé Heat perfume. Then a toddler wanders in, stares at you in horror, screams and bursts into tears. During lockdown this was an everyday occurrence. Imagine that.

One morning in June I stuck my head out of the kitchen door. 'Rose, they've just announced on the radio that the schools are reopening.'

Rose was sitting in the garden watching the children.

'Oh my God, that's brilliant! Tommy, are you crying? Has it been that bad?' she said.

'No, it's not that, it's the Beyoncé Heat perfume. But yes, the kids are going back to school – we're saved!' I said.

In June, France was starting to open up again. The markets, now heavily regulated with masks and one-way systems and hand gel, had reopened a month previously. And so I began back at the market in Richelieu. It was very calm. The period at the start of summer is always pretty dead, but with each successive market I began to sell more. Old customers began to trickle back. Customers who had rightly stopped buying from me because I'd spent six months making shit beer. They were coming back purely on the basis that my beer was good. Maybe I should have just focused on making good beer all along. I wasn't selling enough, but it was promising. In June they opened up the bars and restaurants and schools, and this was the signal for people to emerge from their houses.

I saw old friends. Ali and David stopped by my stall for

a chat. It reminded me of when we first moved over and life was so easy. We'd have long dinner parties. We'd go to restaurants together (read the first book, you cheap bastards). We hadn't spent any time with them for years.

'You really must come over,' I said.

'OK, yes, that would be nice,' said Ali.

'No, you *really* must,' I said desperately.

'OK Tommy,' said David. 'We'll drop by.'

I hoped they would.

The markets picked up, but it's not the way to earn a living. I knew that now. I needed to be selling in big quantities to shops and bars and the like. Instead of focusing on markets and fêtes, I spent more time going round to shops and bars to see if they would stock my beer. There were encouraging signs. A coffee shop in Châtellerault started to stock my beer. A local grocer's in Thuré placed an order as well. The government payments stopped because we were now earning more from the beer. It wasn't enough, though. The bottle company were phoning me. I didn't answer. I needed a really big order. I needed one worth thousands.

'Hi, Tommy, it's Caroline from the Château du Rivau.'

The Château du Rivau is a grand old castle on the way to Chinon. It's open to the public. It has a restaurant that sells salads and vegetables that have been grown in their gardens. It has history. Joan of Arc stayed there. It was originally owned by a family who had connections to the kings of France since the fifteenth century.

'God, really? Good afternoon, Your Highness.' I was startled. Caroline was the daughter of the owner of the château.

'Caroline will do. Do you have beers available to buy? We'd like to stock some for our restaurant.'

'Yes, no problem. I have my new Richard Pils, a beer made with local saffron, I have a Tonka Milk Stout and I have the Berger Blonde.'

'OK, we'll take four hundred bottles of the Berger Blonde and four hundred of the saffron beer. And then we'll take another four hundred in a month's time. But we need the first delivery before the weekend after next. We have a jousting competition at the château. It will be really busy, so we must have it for that.'

'No problem at all, Your Eminence. Thank you for your order.' I curtsied. Shit! Eight hundred bottles of beer. That was exactly the order I was talking about. That was thousands of euros!

I had the beer, that was for sure, and it was good beer. And at a restaurant like that, a really super restaurant that was always busy, I would get noticed. I was sure this would bring in even more orders. The only thing I didn't have were the labels. Luckily there was plenty of time to get them printed and delivered.

CHAPTER 12

My favourite *tarte du vigneron* was eaten in among the vines at Cravant-les-Côteaux. *Tarte du vigneron* comes from Chinon. It's a thin layer of puff pastry with sliced apples covered by a sweet-and-sour, sticky red-wine glaze. You should always take a *tarte du vigneron* on a picnic along with *poire tapée* if you can get over its testicular appearance.

We had just returned to Chinon after a morning out on the bikes when disaster almost struck. I'd pulled up on my bike towing the kids' trailer to where our car was parked in the main square. The car parked next to us didn't see the kids' trailer that had just arrived behind it and he began to reverse out.

'Shit, STOP! *ARRÊTE!*' I shouted. The driver heard me and hit the brakes just as the bumper of his car started to press against the trailer.

'My babies!' I ran to the trailer. 'Oh, thank God. They're all right.'

I moved the trailer out of the way and the driver, white as a sheet, reversed out sheepishly and was on his way as I shook my head condescendingly. I checked the contents of the trailer again to make sure. Not a single bottle was broken. A close-run thing.

For the first time in three months, the kids were at crèche and school all day, so we decided to take advantage of our new freedom. The first real time Rose and I'd been able to get away on our own since we'd had Albert four years ago.

We went on a wine-tasting expedition for the day. The kids hated that trailer, you know. We took them out cycling once in it on the Île de Ré, and they waited till we were the furthest point from the campsite – a good couple of hours – and then began to scream and hit each other. They screamed all the way back and they've refused to set foot in it since. The thing about going on holiday with young children is there's no part of it that isn't stressful. The more something should be relaxing – bike rides, dinner out – the more stressful young children make it. You're really better off staying at home.

The bike trailer was therefore redundant for several months until this day, when we realised that it solved one of the biggest logistical problems mankind has faced: where to put your boxes of wine when you go wine-tasting on bicycles.

It was an alarming 34° C when we drove to Chinon with the bikes on the back of the car and the trailer in the boot that morning. We unloaded the trailer and attached it to my bike and we set off cycling along the D21 towards Cravant-les-Côteaux. The D21 follows the Vienne sixteen kilometres to L'Île-Bouchard through some of the best wine country in France. Cravant-les-Côteaux is one of the main wine-producing villages. It consists of one long road along the bottom of a *falaise*, which is peppered with *vignerons*. More than you could visit in a month. On one side of the road the scenery rises and there are little parcels of vineyards dotted among forest, and on the other side larger vineyards on flat lands stretch down several kilometres to the banks of the River Vienne.

The D21 is quite a busy road, but after twenty minutes or so you turn off to the right and then you can wind your way through the vines on little single-lane roads, covered in squashed grapes and lizards that flit across the tarmac in front of your wheels, without seeing another car. We rolled along this route through the vines, parallel with the D21, for an hour or so until we decided we were probably somewhere near Cravant-les-Côteaux, so we headed back up to the main road to find a *vigneron*.

Some of the wine makers were closed as it was lunchtime, but Patrick Lambert was open for business. I have drunk enough wine now to know quite a few of the local producers, but I'd never come across Patrick Lambert's wine. He invited us into his *cave* – a cellar three metres wide and a couple of metres high dug out of the cliff – and started uncorking bottles for us to taste. The *cave* extended back for a hundred metres, with barrels sitting on their sides to the left and right, spaced evenly all the way to the back, with a path running through the middle of them. Even though we'd only been cycling for an hour or so, we were overheating. The cave was mercifully cool. Patrick reckons it doesn't get hotter than 14° C in there. We drank wine and talked.

Patrick Lambert is a good guy. He's probably quite old, but the wine has preserved him well. He has the look of a man who has worked in the open air for all his life – tanned, creases and folds across his face. Thin and healthy-looking, thick black hair. He's a small producer and he has no desire to be anything more. He hand-picks his grapes, and he uses all-traditional methods. Some modern *vignerons* now heat their grape juice up to sterilise it and then cool it down and add yeast in the same way one might make beer, but Patrick uses the natural yeast that's already on the grape skins to ferment his wine. He has three red wines – a fruity red, a heavier red made with grapes from old vines, and a really super luxurious red that comes from parcels of grapes up on the hills – I think this is fairly typical of Chinon producers (the vineyards in Cravant come under the Chinon wine denomination).

There are various different factors involved in making different styles of wines. For a fruity wine you use younger vines, as the roots don't go so deep. Older vines have deeper roots, so they will pick up more minerally flavours from the earth. Also, to get a fruitier wine, you don't macerate the wine with the skins and pips for as long as you would a heavier wine. This means you get fewer tannins. For his heavier wines he leaves them in oak barrels for a year or a year and a half. Newer oak barrels will give a greater and different flavour from old ones. Patrick told us all of this while pouring us glass after glass of wine. It's funny, I'm normally incapable of retaining any information, but when people talk about booze, it sticks. And so we passed a fabulous hour in his cave. His wine was really superb. The reason I'd not seen it before was because he doesn't sell it to shops or restaurants. You can only get it if you go directly to him. We bought a mixed case of his reds and a box of rosé. Chinon rosé is excellent, you know. The *vignerons* don't think much of rosé – Patrick told us to fill our water bottles up with it for the cycle home – but for me a good Chinon rosé is a match for nearly any other you'll find in France. Dry and crisp, exactly what you want on a hot day, not like those sweet ones you get from Angers or the fruity Provençal rosés. We loaded the kids' trailer up with our bottles, wished Patrick a wobbly good day and rode off to find a picnic spot in the vines to eat our *tarte du vigneron*.

I hadn't done something like that with Rose since our honeymoon. Just the two of us for a few hours, riding around the vines. You have to do that stuff. What's the point of moving to France if you never leave the house? If you never have any fun? But we hadn't had the opportunity to do things like that for what seemed like years. We'd been so busy. We'd been in a war with that brewery and those children, and until now we'd always had at least one child at home. Our French friends have family to lean on. They can give their kids to their grandparents for the weekend and go off and do something nice – but we didn't have that. It was just me and Rose. And then the lockdown happened, and it meant we had the two kids with us at the house for three months. It was no wonder we'd started to turn on each other. But now, with the children back at school and crèche, just to do something as simple as riding bikes through the vineyards together felt like it had gone a long way to repairing us.

We cycled to the Auberge de Crissay for lunch and got a table on the grass.

'The thing is, Rose, I want you to come in with me on the brewery. I need your help,' I said as soon as we sat down. I'd been preparing to tell her that the whole morning, but it still stuck in my throat.

I'm absolutely hopeless at asking people for help. I'd prefer to stick it out, endure whatever I have to endure, and find a way to squirm out of it on my own so I can avoid the shame of other people seeing the intricacies, the depths I have sunk to, but I couldn't get out of this one. And Rose knew the depths I'd sunk to whether she said it or not, because she'd been living alongside it. She'd seen the state of that brewery.

Our *rillons* arrived – a local speciality – hunks of pork belly cooked in lard, local white wine and *arôme Patrelle*, a sort of onion stock, along with a carafe of rosé.

The Auberge de Crissay in Crissay-sur-Manse is one of our favourite places. You eat outside on the grass opposite the Auberge under the shade of an old fig tree. It has a view from the top of the shallow, wide, flat-bottomed valley banked on both sides with fields of wheat and corn that meet down at the banks of the little River Manse, tiptoeing right through the middle of this magnificent setting almost unnoticed.

The food is good here. It's not stuffy – a selection of salads (the best is Touraine salad – a salad with hot potatoes and goat's cheese) and expertly cooked French staples: *entrecôte* – fatty, gristly and flavoursome, or *andouillette* – all the sights sounds, smells and flavours of a farmyard squashed into a tripe sausage. *Andouillette* is not for the faint-hearted. They could get away with charging three times as much as they do at the Auberge de Crissay because of the view, and when it's relaxed like this, it brings the best out of the scenery. Everything's in harmony. Sounded like a tit again there, but if it was all silver service and four different serving staff buzzing around you all the time, you wouldn't be able to relax.

The Auberge rests in the shadow of the old, never to be completed Château de Crissay. To eat there with grass under your feet, above the valley, that scene unfolding beneath you, farms dotted in the distance, a fresh breeze and the shade of the old fig tree to keep you cool even on the hottest days – you know, I don't think there's anywhere better.

'OK Tommy. I'd like that,' said Rose.

I'm so haphazard and Rose is so organised: it was what I'd been craving in that brewery. If I couldn't turn it around on my own, I knew Rose could.

The day before, Rose had helped me bottle the new Sang de Braslou IPA. Bottling had never gone so well; we put systems in place. Before we did anything, we gave the place a good clean down. It was still a pit of slime, but it was an improvement. The beer was the clearest I'd ever managed out of the fermenter. It tasted really super, but more than that, it was well made. It tasted pure. No sourness that stays at the back of your mouth, no other undesirable flavours. We'd have to see how it came out after a couple of weeks in the bottle. I felt so optimistic, and I hadn't felt like that since the summer of 2018, when I was printing obscene slogans on the van. For the first time since I started the brewery, I think we'd left it in a better state at the end of the day than we'd started in the morning.

You've got to let people in. At least a little bit. Paul Burrell taught me that. Charles had shut Diana out when all she wanted to do was love him. I'd been shutting Rose out of the brewery. I'd been dismissing Rose's ideas, turning down her help for years now, because I was too proud to take her help. I was fearful that I'd be pushed aside and at the same time I had this self-defeating glitch within me, and on some level I knew if I let her in, she wouldn't let me run everything into the ground. I wanted to get out of the mess myself, but the truth was, I couldn't. It was clear that the only way this could work was if I had someone with me who's going to combat my worst traits, and there she was, right beside me all that time. Ah, isn't that nice? What a lovely sentiment. Oh, piss off.

When we arrived home there was a parcel at the gate. 'Tommy – the labels have arrived!' Rose held up a cardboard box, which I hacked open with a kitchen knife.

'Ah, crap. They've only sent the Richard Pils labels. What about the Berger Blondes?' This was so typical of that bloody company.

'You'd better speak to them. There's still plenty of time,' said Rose. She was right. No need to panic.

On first glance, the Richard Pils labels were super. I'd changed the label style. Before, the labels took up most of the bottle. Now they ran round the bottom of the bottle like ribbons.

'Tommy, did you mean to make the writing this small?' Rose stuck a label onto an empty bottle to look at it. The brand, *BRASLOU BIÈRE*, looked great in gold, but the writing underneath, where it said Richard Pils, was tiny. It was almost illegible.

'Yes, *Rose*. Of course I did,' I lied. I had to think on my feet or Rose would think I was a total fool.

'But you can't actually read it, Tommy.'

'Yes, it's supposed to be like that. It's a classic brewer's trick, *Rose*. It draws you in.'

'Yes, but you can't actually read it, Tommy. It's so small you can't actually read it. Nobody will know what it is.'

'IT DRAWS YOU IN!'

Trying to find out what had happened to the other labels was frustrating. The online labelling company's customer-service procedure was designed, I think, by the same guy who did the roundabout by the supermarket in Chaveignes. I was constantly finding phone lines going dead, emails not answered, and so on. Eventually I discovered that they'd been printed and were en route to being delivered. They were coming from Italy, but there'd been a hold-up. I would have to speak to the delivery company for more information.

I checked the online tracking on the delivery company's website. All it said was that the labels were in a warehouse somewhere in the middle of Italy. According to the timeline on the page, they'd been there for a week.

When I called the delivery company, it was a nightmare. They would put me through to customer-service departments in the wrong country. If I managed to get through to speak to somebody, they would simply read the internet page that I was already looking at back to me. Finally, one man – I don't know your name, but if you ever read this, you are invited to be my best man at our renewal of vows ceremony – spoke some truths to me.

'Aha, yes, there's a strike in Italy,' said my new best man.

'There's a what?' I replied.

'The Italian branch of our delivery company is on strike,' he said.

'About what?' I said.

'I'm not sure. It could be any number of things. That's why your package hasn't moved for a week.'

'Well, how long will the strike last?'

'It's hard to say. It depends how they are feeling, I guess.'

'But there must be some kind of legislation. They can't strike for ever.'

'They could. That's Italians for you.'

'Those shitting Italians! I take it all back. They need some

209

discipline in their lives. There are rules. They have to follow the rules. For Christ's sake. Those absolute bastards. Can't you make them follow the rules?'

'Is there anything else I can help you with?'

'No. Thank you for your time.'

Suddenly I hated that guy in the clapped-out yellow Fiat following the ambulance down that Italian motorway.

There was a week to go till I needed to deliver the beers. All I had was this internet page where I could track my package. It was easy to track because it wasn't going anywhere.

I checked that page so many times. At the same time, I was fending off calls from the bottle company, until one day a man from a different office called and left a message. He was from a collection agency.

Now at night I would wake up at the slightest noise. Was that the creak of the front gate? Was that the bailiffs here to steal my brewery? It wasn't. They don't operate like that. I was getting confused with ninjas, but it was an extremely tense week. Finally, the Wednesday before the joust, I checked the website and there was movement. The package was in transit again!

I tried to get in touch with the delivery company to find out if they'd get it to me on time. I had nothing for two days. First thing on the Friday morning, the day I was due to deliver, I received an email from the delivery company. The labels, they assured me, would arrive the following Monday. That was the Monday after the jousting competition. It was too late. That was the end of it. I looked at Diana rolling across the kitchen floor like a yoga ball with ears, like a buoy from a shipping lane, and I sank my face into my hands. Perhaps a minute later, Diana started barking. There was someone at the gate.

'Shit. Is that the bailiffs, Diana?'

I peered through the curtains. It didn't look like bailiffs. It looked like a delivery driver. Perhaps it was a trick. Or perhaps it was something Rose had ordered – a new animal maybe, as part of her latest pregnancy cravings. I went gingerly to the gate. The guy handed me a box. On top of the box they'd stuck a label. A beer label – *Berger Blonde*, it said. I tried to hug the delivery driver, but he wisely hopped back into his cab.

'I love you!' I cried. 'You will always be in my heart,' I said solemnly as he disappeared down the road at maximum revs, no doubt to tell someone about his ordeal. The labels had arrived early! It was no surprise the delivery company had got the delivery date wrong. They'd screwed everything else up, so why not? There was no time to lose. I could still get the labels on the bottles and deliver them by late afternoon. Before I'd even got back to the house, the dogs went crazy again. Another car had pulled up.

'Shit. Bailiffs.'

Two gentle-looking French ladies, a mother and daughter, were standing at the gate. They didn't look like bailiffs either.

'Hi there, we're here for the sheep. We're not disturbing you, are we?'

I'd totally forgotten that today was the day we'd agreed they'd come to pick up Bella the sheep. I should have already had it corralled and tied up to a post or something, but instead it was just roaming around the grounds and I had no idea how we'd catch it. I certainly didn't have the time to spend the day chasing a sheep around. I should have told them to go home, that right now my entire life and the lives of my family were on the line. The only thing that was really crucial was to get those labels on the bottles and make the delivery, because it was still possible if I acted now. So instead I did what I've done throughout my life when victory is in sight. As the words came out of my mouth, I realised what I was doing, but it was too late. I hit the self-destruct button. After everything I'd been through in the last year, all the bullshit self-discovery, it turned out I was still that same old twat, determined to sabotage any chance of happiness.

'OK, yes no problem. No, you're not disturbing me. Come in. So how are we going to catch her?' They looked at me blankly. When they'd answered the advert, I'd assumed they'd be farming types. I assumed everyone round here knew how to catch farm animals. I expected them to turn up with a lasso or to make a high-pitched whistle that would draw the sheep to them. They did none of these things. It seemed they expected me to catch my own sheep.

I had caught Bella once before, many months ago, when we had to give her worming potion. Vets may not call it a potion. I'd managed to catch Bella by fooling her into thinking I was her friend by following her around with a handful of grain. Then, before she could see the treachery, I hooked a leg.

'Shit, I've got her!' I cried. 'Rose! What do I do, Rose?' I always think Rose knows what to do when it comes to animals. She used to live with a vet.

'FLIP HER OVER! SIT ON HER! SIT ON HER!' screamed Rose from the other side of the fence, a baby Margot in her arms, Albert beside her, watching with fascination.

I managed to wrestle Bella onto her back and I straddled her.

'Are you sure this is what I'm supposed to be doing?' I said. Bella didn't seem particularly prone.

'I don't know,' said Rose, somewhat disappointingly. 'It seemed like a good idea.'

'You don't know?' Bella freed her back legs and began kicking furiously at my crotch. 'No Bella, NOOOOOOO!'

She's never trusted me since. For future information, you're not supposed to sit on sheep. I looked it up on YouTube afterwards. You're supposed to rock them back onto their hips so they're sitting upright. If you can get them into that position, they become passive. They'll just sit there. That's what sheep shearers do when they shear them. But I couldn't get near Bella now, because she thought I would sit on her again and she didn't want that.

Rose and I chased Bella around the garden for forty-five minutes while the French ladies looked on, stony-faced. Every one of those minutes counted as four bottles not getting labelled. We couldn't get near her. Things were getting desperate.

At one point I cornered Bella and our eyes met. '*Et tu*, Bella?' I said and for a moment I was pleased with myself. But then she darted beyond my grasp and I remembered I had 400 bottles to label and I was running out of time. We needed help. Diana took the opportunity to piss on the French women's car. Albert pulled his trousers down and began weeing in the middle of the lawn and instinctively I knew what I had to do.

'Aha! Um, I think I heard my neighbour over the road. I'll see if he can help,' I explained to Rose and the French ladies. I hadn't heard my neighbour. Diana and Albert had given me an idea. An idea so outrageous that I couldn't tell Rose and I certainly couldn't tell the women who were

213

here for the sheep. And I definitely couldn't let them see what I was doing.

I went out of our gate, walked round to the wall that runs along the road so I was out of their sight, and I pissed up against the wall, and as I pissed I imagined my scent saying 'Help me, somebody. Anybody. I need to label four hundred bottles of beer, but we've got a rogue Cameroonian sheep and if I don't catch it, the bailiffs will come and take everything.'

I went back to the garden and waited. The women wondered what I was doing. Who would answer the call of my scent (great album title)? Now, I shit you not, within three or four minutes of me pissing up against the wall, a car pulled up. David and Ali, our old friends, got out.

'We were passing and thought we'd pop by to see how you guys are. Everything all right?' said David.

Was it coincidence? Maybe. Did he mention that he'd responded to my scent? No, he didn't. Had he arrived at the exact time I needed someone, more than anything, to come and help me in all my life, just after I'd pissed up a wall? Yes, he had. If you don't believe in scenting, then that's up to you, but I am a convert.

David and Ali joined the chase, but even with the extra help, we couldn't catch the sheep until I came up with a frankly brilliant plan. Bella always followed Gadget, the poor thing. That had been the cause of so much misery and yet, ironically, it could now be the path to her freedom. The plan was to create a corridor between our two parked cars. Then we'd lead Gadget between the cars and when Bella followed him, as she inevitably would, we'd block off the corridor behind her and I would jump in between her and Gadget. Thus, she would be trapped in the car corridor.

The plan worked perfectly. Bella dutifully followed Gadget between the cars; David stood to the side of the car with a pallet. I jumped in front of Bella as Rose led Gadget away and there, suddenly, I was face to face with a startled Cameroonian sheep. I realised that I hadn't planned for what I would do once she was actually trapped. Her first instinct was to bolt back the way she had come, but now David had successfully blocked off the route with the pallet. She turned once more to face me. I could feel her Cameroonian breath against my cheek. Then Bella did what I hadn't expected. She charged at me and leapt headfirst into my chest. I flew backwards onto my arse, and she bounced off me and flew backwards onto her arse, sitting upright on her hips in the exact position I'd seen on YouTube. Bella was completely still. It was true: if you get a sheep up on its bum like that, it just sits there. The problem was, it was true of me as well. *This is why I have underachieved all my life. Too much sitting on my arse*, I thought. We both sat and stared at each other. Then something swelled and frothed within me. Something extraordinary was happening. Everything boiled up into one moment. Before Bella could move, I jumped up.

'THE SECOND CHILD ISN'T EASIER THAN THE FIRST!' I screamed as I flexed my biceps to the sun. Bella was shocked. Probably everyone was shocked. Before she could regain her composure, I grabbed Bella in a bear hug, hoisted her up into the air and instinctively began my World's Strongest Man waddle, roaring. The roar of the Moon Tiger.

Bella wasn't done. She found her courage and began kicking and bleating at me, but this was my moment, this was the final Atlas stone in Bermuda or Kenya, or wherever they hold these strong-man events, and I waddled with absolute conviction, roaring when appropriate. The Frenchwomen, definitely startled by the events unfolding, were sharp-witted enough to open the boot of their car, and I threw Bella in. I threw her in, reader, and I roared again as I slammed the boot. Money was exchanged very quickly, and the French women sped off down the road – probably to tell someone about their ordeal. I cared not. I thanked David and Ali, who weren't in the least surprised at the turn of events – they'd known me for some time now – and Rose and I ran back inside to begin our labelling and packaging. Four hundred bottles on my rickety old labelling machine. There might still be time.

CHAPTER 13

'Hi, guys, thanks for coming. Appreciate you rearranging your diaries for this meeting. We'll make it quick, because Damien and Celia are coming over for lunch and I need to get on with my beer stew.'

'Tommy, we are just having breakfast. This isn't a meeting,' said Rose.

'Good. No, you're right. It's an informal synapse mist. Albert – you'll take notes, seeing as you are already drawing on the table.'

'Ah Daddy,' said Albert earnestly, 'you're a big lighthouse poo.'

'Good. OK, right, with the success of the beer at the Château du Rivau, we've got to capitalise on our brand recognition. It's time to start moving into merchandise. I've already had some bespoke Braslou Bière beer glasses made up – here they are.' I handed one each to Rose and Albert. Margot would have thrown it at the wall, so I avoided giving her one. We had managed to label and deliver the beer to the Château du Rivau just in time that Friday in late June when we captured Bella the Cameroonian sheep, I had paid off the bottle company before the bailiffs arrived, and ever since then, the Château du Rivau had been ordering beer by the hundreds. Now it was July and the markets were bustling. The beer was coming out beautifully and we were selling better than ever before. We were firmly in profit.

'Hey, they look really good!' said Rose. It was a large, tulip-shaped beer glass with the Braslou Bière brand proudly in gold and the strapline written in elegant script beneath it. 'Wait a minute, what does the strapline say? *BRASLOU BIÈRE – not dishwasher friendly.* That's the strapline? Not dishwasher friendly? That's our message? Did you mean to have that there?'

'Of course I did, *Rose*,' I lied. That was supposed to be printed under the base of the glass in minute lettering. 'It's an extremely practical piece of advice. The gold will come off if you put them in the dishwasher, and it fits in with our brand values.'

'Which are?'

'We're not dishwasher friendly. It's *meta*. Look, we need to move on. Margot? Any thoughts?' Margot looked at me intensely, as if she was about to say something profound. 'Margot, have you just done a poo?' I said.

'NO!' shouted Margot. 'YES.'

'OK, other ideas for merchandise, just throw them out there.'

'Err, Daddy,' said Albert, gravely, 'you're a sock of the house.'

'OK, look, it's time to drop the bombshell. I've been thinking about our long-term strategy, and I've had a truly brilliant idea. I've decided we are going to become the first brewery that is beer-neutral. It's groundbreaking. It's going to shake up the brewing world like never before.'

'What is a beer-neutral brewery?' Rose asked, despite clearly wishing she hadn't.

'OK, well, we are going to start selling more and more merchandise and less and less beer until finally we will be the first brewery to sell nothing but merchandise.'

'What? And no beer?'

'Yep, a non-brewing brewery. Think about it – merchandise is so much easier. Someone else makes it somewhere in a big factory with quality controls and things. No off flavours – no wading around in old hops and yeast. All we have do to is sell it,' I said. Rose had misgivings, I could see from her face. I thought it best to continue:

'OK, ideas for merchandise. I'm just brain-turding here: berets, lampshades, hot-air balloons, err, trousers for cats, condoms, car keys, shotgun cartridges, um, budgerigars, syringes – just say anything, guys, it's an ideas barbecue – religious candles, birds' nests, curtains, colostomy bags, dog treats—'

'Err, Daddy' said Albert firmly, 'you're a hot-air condom. You're a colostomy.'

'OK, good. Thanks Albert. Any other business?'

I scanned my family, my team, with pride. We'd done it at last.

'Tommy, I want us to move to Cornwall,' said Rose.

'Yes, absolutely. What? You want to what?'

'I don't like it here. I've had enough of the language. I'm sick of us struggling with this brewery and I miss my family. We've hardly seen them in a year with this lockdown.'

'Yes, but this whole global pandemic thing is a one-off, Rose. Don't worry, once we're back to normal, people will be able to visit again.'

'They're already talking about a second wave, Tommy.

What if we get locked down again? What if Covid doesn't go away? Or something else comes along?' She was right, of course. The one thing this pandemic had shown us was how vulnerable our society really is. 'I want us to move to Cornwall. I need to be closer to my family,' said Rose.

'Ah. Right. Cornwall? Yes, well, What? Absolutely not. We can't, Rose. Not now! Are you serious?'

'Yes, I am serious. I want to move back to the UK.'

'But the brewery is about to take off! We're going to go intergalactic, Rose – we just need to hang in there for another few months, can't you see that? There's just no way we can go home now.' It felt like the ceiling was falling in on me. I could hardly breathe. I got up and walked out of the front door into the garden. I could see the forest through the iron railings at the end of the garden. I loved that forest. This was my home. I mean, how could she even consider that after everything we'd been through to get here? And suddenly I heard myself back, promising a better future, and I realised that was the same thing I'd been saying for the last five years. Even if this time I did truly believe that it was about to finally take off because everything was in place, at the same time I could see in Rose's eyes that she'd heard it once too often. And whereas I'd been under all this pressure and a lot of this time in France had been a comprehensive nightmare, at the same time it was an extraordinary adventure for me. I'd really been living, you know what I mean? I'd been making beer and meeting all these people and I just assumed that she'd been really living with me, but now it dawned on me that perhaps she had been living a completely different existence. Little pieces of the puzzle came together. Every time she went to the UK to see her family, she came back depressed. When I was at the fêtes, I'd see her in the corner of my eye with the kids standing to one side while I chatted with all my new friends, but she didn't get to chat with lots of new friends. After twenty minutes she'd have to cart the kids off, screaming and crying, back into the car and head back to the empty house. In fact, she'd hardly left the house since the children arrived. The language was difficult, she'd had no support other than me, especially once Covid-19 hit and none of our family could come over. And she was right about Covid. We didn't know what was going to happen. In the last year France had become a lot further away from the UK than it used to be. The threat of Brexit had been really hard on her and it was true, we never seemed to have any money, and when I looked back into the kitchen to see her sitting at that table, it was clear that she'd had all that she could take.

I could breathe again. I went back in.

'It might be fine for you here, but I want to go back to England. I can't understand what the teachers are saying to me about my child, Tommy. What are we going to do when they need help with their homework? And I can't get a job to help out with the money, because I can't speak good enough French and I just don't think I can learn it. Not to a high enough level,' said Rose.

Oh God. I'd assumed she was loving French life as much as me, but now I realised she was only here because I was here and she wasn't ever going to be happy here. And I thought about Padstow in Cornwall and I knew that, as much as I didn't want to leave Braslou, I could be happy there.

'Ah, crap. OK, Rose.' We hugged and all of a sudden she had the air of lightness and relief. I hadn't seen her like that for months. God, maybe years. It was obvious we had to go. Trying to keep her here would have effectively turned into a hostage situation.

'Ah crap, crap, crap. OK, guys. Fine. I can't believe I'm saying this, but it looks like we're going to Cornwall. OK, marketing meeting – this calls for a whole new marketing campaign. Imagine ideas were butterflies and we are catching them in a net. Let's go. Albert – what's our campaign?'

'Daddy, erm. You have a spotty bottom, Daddy?'

'OK. Thanks, Albert. Right, let me think about this. OK, how about this: "Braslou Bière Is Coming to Cornwall".' I looked up to the heavens and gestured my hand across as I spoke, as if the very words were being written in the sky. I looked at Rose. She seemed into it. I continued, 'And then, underneath, it will say, "Lock Up Your Functioning Alcoholics".'

'It needs work, Tommy,' said Rose.

TOM MATHEWS'
BEER INFUSED RECIPES

We'd had lots of visitors to the brewery over the course of our time here, some of whom were a right pain in the arse. They'd turn up at any hour expecting a full tasting, so you'd open several bottles of beer and then they'd buy one bottle and leave. But when Tom Mathews came over it was always a pleasure. When I first started doing the market in Richelieu, Jean, a woman I'd often see there who had retired in France, kept telling me about her son Tom, who was a chef in London and wanted to come and visit the brewery next time he was over to see her, and I was like, 'Whatever, dude, I'm so on-trend right now.' But when I finally met Tom, I loved the guy. He was a chef, but he was really interested in beer. He wanted to know about how different hops and malt affected the beer. I pretended I knew, and our friendship grew. I've got something in common with Tom, but I don't know what it is. You ever have friends like that?

We'd see him and his partner Sian every summer. They were a power couple. Nowadays they run the extremely successful Chatsworth Bakehouse in Croydon, but back then Tom was working as a chef doing pop-up restaurants and Sian was a producer.

We sat under the trees and drank. One day he said to me, 'I've been using your beers in some of my recipes.'

'And I've been using some of your recipes in my beers,' I replied.

'Really?'

'Um, no.' I hadn't wanted to be outdone, but the jig was up.

'Well, anyway, I'll send you over a few. See what you think.'

From then on we began cooking his recipes with my beer, and they were brilliant. I give them to you here as Tom gave them to me, with his permission. Check out the Chatsworth Bakehouse, 'where bread is bread and people can love each other in any way they want'. I invented that slogan for them without their approval.

Beers listed are from Braslou Bière, alternatives are suggested and are available from your local microbrewery.

Asparagus with Beurre Bière Blanche

A bit like asparagus and beurre blanche, but beerier.

Serves 4

Ingredients
- 1 bottle of Asperges Bière Blanche, or a good wheat beer
- 1 shallot, finely chopped
- 25 ml Chardonnay vinegar
- 1 pack of butter, cubed
- 80 ml double cream
- Salt and white pepper
- Big bunch of new-season asparagus

1. Pour the beer into a stainless-steel pan, add the shallot and reduce over a high heat until about 100 ml remains. Off the heat, add the vinegar and cream and then gradually whisk in the butter to make a glossy sauce. Season well with salt and white pepper. Keep warm.
2. Bring a large pan of salted water to the boil. Trim the woody ends from the asparagus and blanch for 3 minutes.
3. Arrange the asparagus on a large plate and pour over plenty of the beurre bière blanche sauce . . . and crack another one to drink with it.

Roasted Hake with IPA, Bacon and Spring Cabbage

White fish swimming in beer ...

Serves 2

Ingredients

- 1 small head of spring cabbage, roughly sliced – January King or Savoy work well
- 100 g butter
- Handful of silverskin onions, peeled
- 4 rashers of dry-cured bacon, cut into lardons
- 2 cloves of garlic, sliced as thinly as you can
- 1 bottle of Cardinal IPA or an East Coast IPA
- 200 ml good-quality chicken or vegetable stock
- Salt and black pepper
- Oil
- 2 good-sized chunks of hake, skin on
- Small bunch of chervil, chopped

1. Bring a large pan of salted water to the boil and cook the cabbage for 2 minutes.
2. Meanwhile, heat half of the butter in a wide pan and add the onions, bacon and garlic. Cook over a medium heat until the bacon is crispy and the onions are golden brown, their sugars caramelising on the bottom of the pan. Pour in the beer and reduce by half, then add the stock and cabbage and season well with salt and plenty of black pepper.
3. Heat a heavy-based frying pan over a medium to high heat and add some oil and a bit of

butter. Pat the fish dry, season well and fry skin side down for 5 minutes. The skin should be crisp and the fish nearly cooked through. Flip the fish over and let them finish cooking in the residual heat of the pan for a couple more minutes.

4. At this point the cabbage should have a rich beery liquor. Stir in the remaining butter and add the chervil. Transfer to a plate, place the fish on top and enjoy. Buttered new potatoes or mash would go really well with this.

Lamb Shoulder in Rose Beer with Chickpeas and Harissa

This is loosely based on the Tunisian dish Mermez. Tommy's aromatic Rose Pilsner goes so well with all the sweet onions and spices and makes a delicious gravy ready to be soaked up by cous cous!

Serves 4–6

Ingredients
- 4 large onions, sliced
- 10 cloves of garlic, finely grated
- 3 whole preserved lemons
- 2 cinnamon sticks, snapped in half
- 2 bottles of Rose Pilsner
- 1 tablespoon ground cumin
- 1 tablespoon ground coriander
- 1 teaspoon turmeric
- 1 whole lamb shoulder on the bone
- 2 jars good-quality cooked chickpeas
- Salt and pepper
- Small bunches of mint and flat-leaf parsley, roughly chopped

Harissa Paste
- 10 fresh red chillies
- 2 red peppers, roasted and peeled
- 4 cloves of garlic, grated
- 2 teaspoons sweet smoked paprika
- 2 tablespoons roasted and ground cumin seeds
- 2 tablespoons roasted and ground caraway seeds

- 3 tablespoons good-quality red wine vinegar
- 100 ml extra-virgin olive oil
- Sea salt

1. Preheat the oven to 160° C. Arrange the onions, garlic, preserved lemons and cinnamon sticks over the bottom of a large baking dish. Pour the beer into a large jug and add the remaining spices and stir well to combine. Place the lamb shoulder on top of the onions, season well with salt and pepper and pour over the spiced beer mix. Cover with foil and bake for 3–4 hours.

2. Meanwhile, make the harissa. Add all the ingredients except the olive oil into a food processor (or a pestle and mortar, if you're old school) and reduce to a flame-red pulp. Season well and stir in the olive oil. This will keep for a week in the fridge.

3. After 3–4 hours the lamb should be yielding and the onions and preserved lemons almost dissolved into the beery juice. At this point add in the chickpeas and crank the oven up to 200° C. Cook uncovered for another 30 minutes, allowing the lamb to crisp up and the chickpeas to soak up some of that juice.

4. Bring the whole shoulder to the table and sprinkle over the mint and parsley. Serve with the harissa and a pile of couscous.

IPA-Battered Aubergine, Honey and Tahini Sauce

A great beer snack on a hot day!

Serves 2

Battered Aubergine
- 150 g cornflour
- 100 g self-raising flour
- Large pinch of salt
- 200 ml Cardinal IPA, or an East Coast IPA
- 1 large aubergine
- 1 litre sunflower oil, for frying

Tahini Sauce
- 3 tablespoons tahini paste
- Juice of half a lemon
- Pinch of salt
- 150 ml cold water

To Finish
- Sea salt
- Quality runny honey
- Small bunch of fresh mint, roughly chopped

1. Combine the flours, salt and beer in a large bowl and whisk until just combined. Cut the aubergine into bite-sized chunks and add into the batter.
2. Spoon the tahini into a small bowl, add the lemon juice, salt and gradually whisk in the water to form a smooth, creamy sauce.

3. Heat the oil in a large pan and fry the battered aubergine pieces until crispy and golden, then drain on kitchen paper. Transfer the aubergine to a warm plate, season with sea salt, douse with honey, sprinkle with mint and spoon over the tahini sauce. Get in the garden and gobble down.

Beer-Can Chicken and BBQ IPA Onions

Braslou Bière isn't available in cans but that's no problem, as the beer doesn't add tons of flavour, its main function is to steam the chicken from the inside out with super moist results. Any mass-produced blonde beer in a can would work ...
I used Leffe, but you could try Kronenbourg or Goudale and see which one works best!

Serves 4

Beer-Can Chicken
- 2 tablespoons soft dark brown sugar
- 3 tablespoons sweet smoked paprika
- 2 teaspoons sea salt
- 1 teaspoon celery salt
- 1 teaspoon hot chilli powder
- 1 teaspoon onion powder
- 1 teaspoon mustard powder
- 1 teaspoon garlic powder
- Small handful of fresh thyme leaves
- Good grind of black pepper
- 1 large free-range chicken
- Dash of olive oil
- 1 large can of beer

BBQ IPA Onions
- 6 medium onions, keep whole in their skins
- 2 bottles of Lait de Braslou IPA
- 4 tablespoons soft brown sugar
- Glug of Worcestershire sauce

- 3 tablespoons red wine vinegar
- Big squirt of tomato ketchup

1. Make a Memphis style dry rub for the chicken by combining the brown sugar, paprika, salt, celery salt, chilli, onion, mustard and garlic powders, thyme leaves and pepper in a bowl. Roughly score and oil up the chicken skin and rub the spices liberally all over.

2. Open the can of mass-produced beer and drink a quarter of it. Taste its inferiority. Set the can on an old baking tray. Place the chicken cavity over the can and transfer to the barbecue. Cook with the lid on for approximately 45 mins to an hour. The chicken should be falling apart at the joints, deep smoky coloured and very juicy.

3. Meanwhile, make the IPA BBQ Onions. Add all the ingredients to a large saucepan and bring to the boil. Simmer until the onions are tender, then remove from the beery mix. When cool enough, peel and cut each onion in half and transfer to the barbecue to get charred and gnarly. Continue to reduce the beer mix down to a sticky BBQ sauce.

4. Bring the chicken to the table still sat upright on its can, tear apart and smother in the IPA BBQ sauce. Eat with your hands . . . chicken in one and an onion in the other.

Stout Float

Who wants to cook when it's hot outside? This is a perfect lazy BBQ pudding, like a boozy, beery affogato.

Serves 4

Ingredients

- 2 bottles of Tonka Milk Stout, or any other strong, sweet stout
- 4 large scoops of vanilla ice cream
- Fresh red fruits ... strawberries and cherries are best!

1. Divide the stout between four straight-edged tumblers.
2. Scoop the ice cream onto the stout.
3. Sit in the paddling pool and drink with a plate of cherries. *La belle vie*!

Mouclade and Richard Pils

A classic mussel dish of La Rochelle ... but not quite! This beery version uses Braslou Bière's Richard Pils which is brewed using saffron and is an easy cheat ingredient to bag even more flavour! The saffron marries perfectly with the shellfish and who doesn't like curry and beer?

Serves 2

Ingredients
- Knob of butter
- 1 large onion, chopped
- 2 cloves of garlic, finely grated
- 1 kg live mussels, washed and debearded
- 1 bottle of Braslou Richard Pils (or a good pilsner and a pinch of saffron)
- 2 heaped teaspoons of curry powder
- 100 g full fat crème fraîche
- Squeeze of lemon
- Good grind of black pepper
- Small bunch of parsley, roughly chopped

1. Melt the butter in a large pot or casserole dish, add in the onion and garlic and cook for 5 minutes until soft and sweet. Tip in the mussels and beer, crank the heat to 11 and put the lid on.
2. When the mussels have opened, drain through a colander, catching the juice in a large bowl, discard any that haven't opened. Add the

mussel/beer liquor back into the pot, spoon in the curry powder and boil rapidly for a couple of minutes.

3. When the liquor has reduced slightly and the curry powder lost its raw edge, turn off the heat and whisk in the crème fraîche, lemon juice and black pepper. Tip the mussels back into the pot with the chopped parsley and combine well. Grab some bread and cold Richard, and dig in.

Beery Bò Kho

I love Vietnamese food, and I particularly love *bò kho*. This fragrant stew isn't a million miles away from a classic French *daube de boeuf*, and the added dark beer adds a deep, comforting richness, perfect on a cold day. Stick it in the oven and go for a pint ... and always serve with crusty baguette!

Serves 4

Ingredients
- 6 large shallots
- 1 knob of ginger
- 5 cloves of garlic
- 1 large fresh red chilli
- 1 dried chilli
- 1 large stem of lemongrass, white end only
- 1 kg blade of beef, diced
- 2 bottles of Clifton Porter or any other strong dark beer
- 1 tin of plum tomatoes, drained of their juices
- 1 teaspoon five-spice powder
- 3 star anise
- 2 sticks of cinnamon
- 2 tablespoons fish sauce
- 2 tablespoons brown sugar
- 3 large carrots, peeled and roughly chopped
- 10 waxy new potatoes, peeled
- Small bunch of coriander
- Sea salt and pepper
- Olive oil

1. Firstly, make the paste. Add the shallots, ginger, garlic, chillies and lemongrass to a pestle and mortar or food processor and reduce to an aromatic pulp.

2. Season the beef well with salt and pepper. Heat some oil in a heavy-based ovenproof casserole dish and brown the beef on all sides.

3. When the beef is well browned, add the paste and cook for a further 5–10 minutes to release the sweetness of the shallots.

4. Pour in the dark beer, add the tomatoes, five-spice powder, star anise, cinnamon, fish sauce and brown sugar and bring to a simmer, put the lid on and transfer the dish to the oven and cook at 160° C degrees for 1.5 hours.

5. Go to the pub.

6. When you get back, add the carrots and potatoes to the stew and return to the oven for another 30 minutes.

7. Ladle into large bowls, top with the chopped coriander and eat with a baguette each.

Beer Onion Soup with Stout Rarebit Toast

A French classic seen through beer goggles ... The amber coloured Biscuit Ale brings a deep dried fruit flavour to the soup while the Clifton Porter adds another level of savouriness to the Comte cheese rarebit.

Serves 4

Soup

- 6 large sweet onions, peeled and thinly sliced
- 2 cloves of garlic, finely grated
- 25 ml brandy
- 1 bottle of Biscuit Ale, or a good English bitter
- 500 ml quality beef stock (or vegetable stock)
- 2 tablespoons brown sugar
- Small bunch of fresh thyme and 3 bay leaves tied together
- Dash of sherry vinegar
- Large knob of butter
- Salt and pepper

Rarebit

- 50 g butter
- 1 heaped tablespoon plain flour
- 1 teaspoon Dijon mustard
- 200 ml Clifton Porter
- 500 g Comté, grated
- Pinch of cayenne
- Good glug of Worcestershire sauce
- 4 slices of country bread

1. First make the soup. Melt the butter in a large pot and cook the onions, garlic and herb bundle until the onions are light brown and the sugars are caramelising in the bottom of the pan. At this point, season with salt and pepper and continue to cook for a further 10 minutes, scraping all the bits off the base of the pan.
2. Once the onions are soft and very brown, add the brandy and allow the alcohol to flame off. Then add the sugar and pour in the Biscuit Ale and stock. Leave the soup to simmer for 20 minutes to reduce in volume and intensify in flavour.
3. Meanwhile make the rarebit. Heat the butter in a saucepan and whisk in the flour. Cook this for a minute or so, until brown in colour, then add in the Clifton Porter, Dijon mustard, cayenne and a big splash of Worcestershire sauce. Continue to cook until thickened, then turn off the heat and whisk in the grated Comte.
4. Lightly toast the country bread slices under a grill, then spoon the rarebit mixture over each slice and return to the grill until golden and bubbling. Check the seasoning of the soup and finish with a dash of Sherry vinegar.
5. Remove the herb bundle and ladle the soup into bowls and top with the rarebit toasts.

Loaded Confit Duck Fries with Blonde Ale Pickles and Beer-Soaked Mustard

This is the perfect blotting paper for an afternoon on the beers ... it's ideal for sharing, so serve this on one giant plate with plenty of napkins. Make the ale pickles and beer-soaked mustard at least one day ahead to let the flavours develop. I've used tinned duck confit, but you can make your own if you're inclined.

Serves 4

Blonde Ale Pickles
- 5 ridged cucumbers, sliced thinly
- Sea salt
- 1 bottle of Berger Blonde Ale, or an Abbaye style blonde
- 350 ml cider vinegar
- 200 g caster sugar
- 1 teaspoon black peppercorns
- 1 teaspoon yellow mustard seeds
- Pinch of chilli flakes
- 1 small bunch of dill, roughly chopped

Beer-Soaked Mustard
- 200 g yellow mustard seeds
- 1 bottle of Clifton Porter
- 120 ml cider vinegar
- 3 tablespoons soft brown sugar
- 2 tablespoons honey
- 1 teaspoon turmeric

- ½ teaspoon allspice
- 1 teaspoon sea salt

Confit Duck Fries
- 6 large, dry textured potatoes like Maris Piper or Agria
- 1 tin of confit duck legs in duck fat
- Splash of beer
- Salt and pepper
- 6 whole cloves of garlic, skins on and cracked
- Handful of thyme sprigs

1. Make the pickles. Place the sliced cucumber into a colander and salt well. Leave to drain for 2–3 hours. Combine the rest of the ingredients in a small pan and bring to the boil, then allow to cool completely before adding the cucumbers. You can jar these up and keep them in the fridge for up to a month. They will only get better.
2. Make the mustard. Tip the mustard seeds into a bowl and cover with the beer and vinegar. Cover and refrigerate overnight. The next day, transfer the mustard seed/beer mix to a blender and add the remaining ingredients. Blend on high for about 5 minutes until smooth and thickened nicely. If it's too thick, you can loosen the mustard with a drop more beer.
3. Now make the French fries. Wash the potatoes but leave the skins on. Cut into thick batons and place in pan of cold, salted water. Bring the water to the boil and allow to simmer for 5

minutes. Drain the fries and lay them out on a tray to allow the steam to escape and the potato to fully dry out; this will help make them really crispy.

4. Preheat the oven to 200° C. Separate the duck legs from the fat and place in an ovenproof dish with a splash of beer and roast on the top shelf of the oven for about 45 minutes.

5. Take the duck fat and melt it on a large baking tray. Add the fries and carefully coat in the hot fat, season well with salt and pepper then throw on the garlic cloves and thyme. Roast the fries below the duck legs on the lower shelf of the oven . . . the duck and fries should hopefully become crispy and delicious at the same time!

6. Grab a large sharing dish and pile on the fries and shred the duck flesh and crispy skin all over. Drizzle with the Beer–Soaked Mustard and scatter over the Blonde Ale Pickles.

Ricotta Doughnuts and Hot Chocolate Stout Sauce

There aren't many ingredients that would improve hot chocolate sauce ... there's only one I can think of. Stout. So, hot chocolate stout sauce can't be improved. Fact.

Serves 4

Doughnuts
- 30 g caster sugar, plus an extra 50 g for dusting
- 30 g butter at room temperature
- 250 g ricotta (fresh goat's curd is also really good in this)
- Grated zest of an orange
- 40 g plain flour
- 2 eggs
- 1 teaspoon cinnamon
- 1 litre sunflower oil for deep-frying

Hot Chocolate Stout Sauce
- Bottle of Ported Stout (or a bottle of strong stout and a good dash of port)
- 120 g caster sugar
- 300 g dark chocolate, chopped

1. Add the sugar and soft butter to a mixing bowl and whisk together until pale. Whisk in the ricotta and then the eggs one at a time. Grate in the orange zest and fold in the flour. Cover the bowl and chill the mix in the fridge for an hour.
2. For the sauce, pour the stout and sugar into a saucepan and bring to a simmer. Just before it

boils, turn off the heat, tip in the chocolate and stir until the sauce is smooth and shiny.

3. Mix the extra 50 g of sugar with the cinnamon in a bowl. Heat the oil in a medium-sized pan. Carefully spoon balls of the doughnut mix into the oil until golden brown, about 4 minutes. Drain the doughnuts on kitchen paper and toss in the cinnamon sugar. Eat immediately with the Hot-Chocolate Stout Sauce and a cold Stout Float.

IPA Focaccia with Potatoes and Raclette

IPA focaccia is a revelation. Yeasty bubbles make it super light, while the residual malt sugars caramelise in the oven, giving an amazing crust, and its hoppy character makes cheese taste even cheesier! This recipe makes one massive, party-sized bread.

Serves 6–8

Focaccia dough
- 1 kg strong bread flour
- 20 g dried yeast
- 1 bottle of Sang de Braslou IPA, or a West Coast IPA
- 20 g salt
- 50 ml extra-virgin olive oil, plus extra for greasing
- 350 ml warm water

Topping
- 250 g raclette cheese, sliced
- 1 onion, thinly sliced
- 250 g la Ratte potatoes, peeled, parboiled and sliced
- 2 cloves of garlic, sliced
- 50 ml extra-virgin olive oil plus 20 ml water, whisked to an emulsion
- Sea salt

1. The day before, make the starter. In a large bowl, combine 500 g of the flour with 500 g of water and 10 g of the yeast. Cover and leave overnight.

2. The next day the starter should be nice and bubbly. Pour in the beer, add the remaining yeast, the other 500g of bread flour and the salt. Mix well until smooth, pour in the olive oil and mix until incorporated. Cover and leave to double in size.

3. Stretch the dough over itself, back to front, turn the bowl 90 degrees and stretch again. Repeat this twice more, cover and leave again to rise. This technique helps strengthen the gluten and give an aerated texture to the crumb.

4. Preheat the oven to 220° C. Take a large baking tray, line with greaseproof paper and oil well. Carefully transfer the dough to the tray and leave to bubble up for 30 minutes.

5. Cover the focaccia dough with the raclette, onion, potatoes and garlic slices, pour over the olive-oil emulsion and sprinkle liberally with sea salt.

6. Bake for 45 minutes to an hour. The bread should have a deep-gold top and a crispy bottom. Serve warm with sliced smoked ham and Blonde Ale Pickles (page 241).

ACKNOWLEDGEMENTS

Thanks to the family:

Rose, Albert and Margot, George and Ellen Barnes, Aunty Joan, Uncle Chris, Aunty Maggi, Aunty Myra, David Reynolds

Thanks to my friends:

Tom Mathews, Damien and Celia, Claude and Annie, Christian and Marie Scott and Elena, Rupert and Annabelle, Ali and David, Tia and Stuart, Fred Baty, Claudine the Mayor, Joel Grignon, Benoit from Little Belgique, Ursula Pages, Caroline from Chateau Du Rivau , Nico and all the guys from Richelieu market. Fuck, I'm going to miss that market.

And to the publishing team:

Sarah and Kate Beal, Kate Quarry, Laura Mcfarlane, Fiona Brownlee, David Wardle, Sara Keane

LES RICHELAIS

CHINON
CRAVANT-LES-COTEA
PANZOU
VIENNE
L'ILE BOU
CHAMPIGNY-SU
CHAVEIGNES
LOUDUN
RICHELIEU
BRASL
BRASL
FAYE-LA-VINEUSE